Good Grammar
For Students

SAGE Essential Study Skills

Essential *Study Skills* is a series of books designed to help students and newly qualified professionals to develop their skills, capabilities, attitudes and qualities so that they can apply them intelligently and in ways which will benefit them on their courses and careers. The series includes accessible and user-friendly guides to improving a range of essential life-long skills and abilities in a variety of areas, including:

♦ **writing essays and reports**

♦ **numeracy**

♦ **presenting information**

♦ **and communicating your ideas.**

Essential Study Skills will be an invaluable aid to all students on a range of higher education courses and to professionals who need to make presentations, write effective reports or search for relevant information.

Good Grammar For Students

Howard Jackson

SAGE Publications

London ● Thousand Oaks ● New Delhi

SAGE Publications Ltd
1 Oliver's Yard
55 City Road
London EC1Y 1SP

SAGE Publications Inc.
2455 Teller Road
Thousand Oaks, California 91320

SAGE Publications India Pvt Ltd
B-42, Panchsheel Enclave
Post Box 4109
New Delhi 110 017

British Library Cataloguing in Publication data

A catalogue record for this book is available
from the British Library

ISBN 1-4129-0202-9
ISBN 1-4129-0203-7 (pbk)

Library of Congress Control Number: 2005902146

Typeset by C&M Digitals (P) Ltd., Chennai, India
Printed on paper from sustainable resources
Printed and bound in Great Britain by The Cromwell Press Ltd, Trowbridge, Wiltshire

for Marley,
a representative of
the next generation

Contents

Introduction

If you are a student in further or higher education and you have to write essays or reports for assessment in your course, then this book is designed for you.

Its aim is to enable you to improve the quality and accuracy of your writing. It does this by:

- teaching you something about the basics of the grammar of English — how sentences and texts are structured

- giving you some useful tips on things to look out for and pitfalls to avoid

- pointing out to you where you can go for further information and advice.

While the general tone of this small book is to give you help and advice, the first six chapters are largely about how the grammar of English works, and how you can exploit in your own writing the mechanisms available in English. The next three chapters focus on advice: tips on sentence structure, an examination of computer grammar checkers, help with spelling and punctuation. The final chapter shows where you can go for more detailed advice.

The book contains many examples, illustrating the points being made or highlighting good and bad practice. Some of these examples are made up. In some chapters, the examples are taken from two computer corpora of texts:

- LOB — the Lancaster–Oslo/Bergen one-million-word corpus of 500 extracts from British English publications from the year 1961, representing texts across a range of genres, from journalism through academic to fiction

- FLOB — the Freiburg LOB corpus, parallel to the original LOB, but with extracts from publications from the year 1991.

A few additional authentic examples are taken from other publications, whose sources are indicated.

Whatever academic subject you are studying, you will have had to learn the terminology that is used for talking about that subject. We sometimes pejoratively refer to such technical vocabulary as 'jargon'. Grammar has its jargon too. Jargon can be empowering: it makes you knowledgeable about a subject and able to talk about it intelligently. This book introduces some terms used for talking about language, and about grammar in particular. Those introduced in a chapter are summarised at the end, and there is a Glossary at the end of the book. The Glossary defines the main terms used in the book and also acts as an index, pointing you to the chapter(s) in which a term was mainly used and explained. You might like to look at the Glossary now, to familiarise yourself with what it looks like.

You will find it useful if you study the material in the first six chapters in order, since they build up a picture of English grammar and its resources, and introduce the terminology. My contention in this book is that you can best improve the quality and accuracy of your writing by being aware of the resources available to you and the techniques for exploiting them. You will thus become aware of your own use of language, and you will be able to talk about it and develop a self-critical attitude towards it, thus enabling you to improve on what you write.

Just as a successful painter needs to be knowledgeable about the materials – canvas, paint, brushes – that they use, and the techniques – paint mixing, brush strokes – for exploiting them, so a writer should be knowledgeable about the resources of language – grammar and vocabulary – and the techniques for exploiting them – choice of words, sentence and text structuring. This book is designed to help you to advance your knowledge in this area.

1 What Do We Mean by 'Grammar' – Good and Bad?

If you have picked up this book and started reading it, then either you have been recommended to do so by a tutor, or you feel the need to improve your own writing by finding out more about how sentences and texts are structured. You already have the grammar of English stored in your head: you either acquired it as your first language, or learned it as a second or foreign language. And it serves you very well when you speak. Writing, though, is often a different matter: it demands more careful thought to get it structured right; and you have only one chance to get your meaning across, because your reader can't usually ask you for clarification. So, for written language it helps to be aware of how the grammar works, so that you can make the right choices of words and structures to make your communication as effective as possible.

This first chapter is a ground-clearing exercise. Its aim is to clear out of the way some of the misconceptions that people frequently have about grammar and to propose a more reasonable view of grammar, so that we have an established starting point for the rest of the book.

> **EXERCISE**
>
> At this point, you may find it useful to write down what you think 'grammar' is about. Try and write it as a definition: 'Grammar is ….' Then compare your definition with the discussion that follows.

Say the word 'grammar' to most people and you will more than likely get a negative reaction. Why does the word have such a bad press? For older generations it may stem from hours toiling over tedious grammatical analysis in English lessons at school. For younger generations it is perhaps fear of the unknown and an apprehension that it is something that must be avoided.

While the primary purpose of this book is not to rehabilitate grammar, I hope that you will come to appreciate that a knowledge of the grammar of the language that you speak and write will not only benefit your career as a student, and beyond, but also prove to be not as scary as you had anticipated. Indeed, there are some of us who find the study of language, and of grammar in particular, to be so fascinating that we devote our working lives to it. 'Sad people,' you may say, but the results of their study may yet benefit you and your career.

If you are afraid of grammar, it is probably because you don't know what grammar is about. Many people think of grammar as being primarily about spelling and punctuation, but these relate only to the written form of the language. They have no equivalent in the spoken language, and yet grammar is an essential component of both spoken and written language. Language would not be language without grammar.

Some Misconceptions Examined

1   Grammar is the set of rules for speaking and writing English properly; for example, you should say *we were* and not *we was*.

2   Some languages have more grammar than others; English doesn't have much grammar.

3   Foreigners need to learn grammar when they learn English, but I'm a native speaker and so I don't need to.

4   Grammar is what you find in grammar books. I've never read one. Grammar is for nerds.

5   Grammar is no practical use to anyone except grammarians.

By labelling such statements as 'misconceptions', I have already betrayed that I think they are wrong; so let me explain why I think that.

The first of them is widespread, including among government ministers during the debates in the 1980s and 1990s on English in the national curriculum in schools. This view wants to reduce grammar teaching to a set of simple rules for correcting non-standard or dialect speech. The most often quoted rule was the so-called 'subject–verb' agreement rule, which states that you should say *I was* and *he/she/it was*, but *we were, you were* and *they were*. *I* and *he/she/it* are 'singular' subjects and so should be followed by the singular verb form *was*, while *we, you* and *they* are 'plural' subjects and should be followed by the plural verb form *were*. However, many people say – and it is a question largely of speech, not writing – *we was* and *you was*. One government minister went so far as to suggest that teachers on playground duty should listen out for such 'mistakes' and correct pupils who committed them.

Now, subject–verb agreement is something that grammar is concerned with, but not in this prescriptive way. Grammarians would recognise that different systems, or 'rules', operate in different contexts. People whose local speech form (dialect) has only the form *was*, whether the subject is singular or plural, do not necessarily carry across this 'rule' to formal writing. In saying this, you might notice that I'm trying to change the meaning of the term 'rule'. For grammarians, a rule is not a prescription of language that must be obeyed; rather it is a convention by which we structure the sentences and utterances of our language. Grammatical rules vary from one variety of language or context of language use to another: speech is different in grammar from writing; teenage speech is different from adult speech; speech at the social club is different from speech at an academic conference. And sometimes a rule is variable anyway.

EXERCISE

Insert *was* or *were* in the following sentences:

1 Aston Villa _____ a great football team.
2 The band _____ exhausted by the end of the gig.
3 England _____ facing defeat yet again.
4 The government _____ proposing to charge students higher fees.

Normally you don't think whether to use *was* or *were*; it's instinctive. But in these examples both are possible; so, does it make any difference which you use? Arguably, using singular *was* means that you are regarding *Aston Villa, the band, England* and *the government* as single, undifferentiated entities; whereas using plural *were* implies that you regard them as groups of individuals.

Grammatical rules also change over time, even for a given variety of English. Let me give you two examples. You may have noticed that I used the preposition *from* after the adjective *different* at the end of the paragraph before the exercise. That probably marks me as being rather old-fashioned. Most people these days would say – and write – *different to*. One is not 'right' and the other 'wrong'; both 'rules' co-exist at the moment. In due course, *different from* may well disappear. My second example concerns the use of *less* and *fewer*.

EXERCISE

Insert either *less* or *fewer* in the following sentence:

There are _____ students in class this week.

My prediction would be that you would choose *less* rather than *fewer*. And I am sure that you would say: 'There is less agreement about how we should dress for a formal occasion.' The 'rule' used to be: use *fewer* with 'countable' nouns (like *student*) and *less* with 'uncountable' nouns (like *agreement* in this context). But the common practice in all varieties of English now seems to be: use *less* whatever noun may follow.

EXERCISE

Now insert either *a large number of* or *a large amount of* in the following sentence:

There was _____ students attending the class this week.

Your response to this one is rather less predictable. A similar and parallel change (to that affecting *fewer/less*) appears to be happening with *a number of* (used with countable nouns) and *an amount of* (used with uncountable nouns), especially if used in the expression *a large number/amount of.*

If you chose *number* here but *less* in the previous example, then your grammar hasn't quite completed the rule change that is taking place in contemporary English.

You may have noticed in our discussion of this first misconception that we have used grammatical terms like 'subject', 'verb', 'noun', 'countable', 'agreement'. You cannot talk about how language works or how language is used without a grammatical terminology. This is the beginning of an answer to misconception 5.

Let us turn to the second misconception: that languages have variable amounts of grammar. This misconception usually arises among people who have had some experience of a highly inflecting language like Latin, Greek or Russian, or even of a moderately inflecting language like German or French. Grammar is here being equated with endings on words, the 'declensions' of nouns and adjectives and the 'conjugations' of verbs. In Latin, for example, every noun has potentially ten different forms, and every verb over a hundred, and the forms may differ according to the 'class' that a noun or verb belongs to. If that is all there is to grammar, then English doesn't have very much:

- a maximum of three endings on a noun — *girl-s* (plural), *girl-'s* (possessive singular), *girl-s'* (possessive plural)

- normally three endings on a verb — *talk-s* (third person singular present tense), *talk-ed* (past tense/past participle), *talk-ing* (present participle)

- two endings on some adjectives — *small-er* (comparative), *small-est* (superlative).

But that isn't all there is to grammar. The kinds of grammatical meaning that are expressed by the endings (inflections) on Latin nouns and verbs are expressed in different ways in a language like English. What becomes more important is the order in which words are sequenced in a sentence and how different groups of words are joined together by items such as prepositions.

Let us turn to the third misconception: that grammar is only for foreign language learners. If English is your first language, or indeed if it is a second language acquired in childhood, then you will not have been taught grammar. Linguists talk of 'language acquisition', and the rules (including the grammar) for speaking English will have been 'internalised' with little conscious effort on your part. If you learn another language as a teenager or adult, then it is not so easy to 'acquire' this second language in the same way that you did your first language. You may well require, and it is often helpful to be told, something about the 'rules' of grammar in the language.

When you started school, if you can remember back that far, you would have been taught to read and write in your first language, and you would have been conscious of the learning effort involved. You would have learned new words, how to spell them, how to pronounce them, how to use them in sentences and texts. You would have learned in due course about the more complex sentence structures, about paragraphs and the structure of different types of text. The learning may have been more by example and correction of misguided efforts than by rule, but it involved learning rather than acquisition. Indeed, your task may have been made easier, if you could have understood how the system worked, and some of your present uncertainty and persistent mistakes could have been avoided by more explicit explanation of what was going on in the grammar of English.

EXERCISE

What is the difference between:

My aunt who lives in Sheffield has sent me a DVD for Christmas

and

My aunt, who lives in Sheffield, has sent me a DVD for Christmas?

I expect you to say: the first sentence implies that I have more than one aunt, and the second that I have only one. In other words, *who lives in Sheffield* 'defines' which aunt I'm referring to in the first sentence, but in the second it's just a bit of extra information that I chose to tell you about my one and only aunt. You mean to tell me that a mere pair of commas makes that vital difference in meaning? Well, yes, it does as a matter of fact. What's going on here? It has to do with a grammatical distinction between 'defining' and 'non-defining' relative clauses (*who lives in Sheffield* is a relative clause), and that presupposes knowing what a relative clause is and does and what 'defining' and 'non-defining' mean.

Unless you put those commas in, and in the right places, you may not be making your meaning clear. This is one of the most common confusions that I come across in all kinds of documents, including students' assignments. If you don't get it right, you'll make it harder for your reader to understand what you are trying to say. Getting it right involves understanding the grammar of relative clauses. So, grammar is for you as well, native speaker!

Let's move on to the fourth misconception: that grammar is only in grammar books and it's only for nerds. First, I hope that our discussion earlier has demonstrated that, as a native speaker of English, you have acquired, or internalised, the grammar of the language, and that whenever you speak or write English you are using the 'rules' of the grammar in order to produce sentences that can be understood by your hearers or readers. So, grammar is not just in grammar books; it's in your head. What's in the grammar book is an attempt at describing what is in our heads, a formulation of the rules by which we construct sentences, texts and discourses in our language.

Second, I hope also to have demonstrated that, especially in the more complex forms of writing, for example relative clauses, a more explicit knowledge of grammar can help in constructing sentences that are clear in the meaning that you wish to convey. Making it difficult for your reader to understand your message may detract from the message itself. So, grammar is not just for nerds; it's for anyone who wants to be a successful communicator, especially in writing.

Finally, let's deal with the fifth misconception: that grammar is of no practical use. I'll take an example from the field of human–computer interaction. If you want to give your computer an instruction or input data into a file, then you currently most probably use a keyboard and a mouse. When you ring up an organisation, a bank or insurance company, for example, and you are answered by a computer, you have to answer the voice at the other end by pressing keys on your telephone's keypad. In due course, both of these interactions with computers will be achieved through your talking to the computer, and it talking back to you. To enable this to happen, the software engineers who are writing the programs that will make this possible not only have to account for the fact that every individual has a different 'voice' but also have to consider that the sentence structures used for a particular instruction will not always be identical. They, therefore, need a means of analysing the grammar of sentences, so that the machine will 'understand' the instructions correctly.

Anyone working in the area of 'natural language processing' needs a detailed knowledge of the way in which grammar works. That also goes for anyone involved in teaching foreign languages, including English as a foreign language, or involved in treating language impairments as a speech and language therapist, or involved in teaching English language and literature, either as a primary school teacher or as a secondary school teacher of English. Arguably, anyone who uses the English language in their professional life – journalists, marketing executives, press officers, public relations people, administrators – as well as those involved in writing reports, and that's probably just about every professional, needs to know about the workings, including and especially the grammar, of the language that they are using to craft their communication. At the least, knowledge of grammar will enable you to be a more discerning, more reflective, more skilled user of the language.

'Bad' Grammar

What, then, is bad grammar? Put simply, bad grammar results when the 'rules' for structuring language appropriate to the variety or context are flouted, such that the reader or listener cannot readily gain the intended meaning or is liable to misunderstand what is written or said. Let me give you a few examples from formal written English.

1 Sitting in the corner, she could not see anyone.

Who is 'sitting in the corner', 'she' or 'anyone'? Taken at face value, a reader would be expected to interpret this sentence as meaning 'because she was sitting in the corner, she couldn't see other people'. However, some people write such sentences and expect to mean 'she couldn't see anyone who might be sitting in the corner'. With 'participle clauses' such as *sitting in the corner* in this example, it is important to make clear which noun or pronoun they relate to. It may be necessary to reword the sentence in order to make it unambiguous; for example, 'She was sitting in the corner and so she could not see anyone.'

2 We don't know whose supposed to be contributing to the publication.

This mistake arises because two words that sound the same in speech – *whose* and *who's* – have two quite different roles in grammar. *Whose* is the 'possessive' form of the relative pronoun *who*; for example in *the student whose name I've forgotten*. *Who's* is a contracted form of *who is* or *who has*; for example in *the member of staff who's (who is) nicknamed 'Tadpole'*. So, our example sentence should have read: *We don't know who's supposed …* .

3 Figure 1 shows that 40% of the population read a newspaper. Whereas Figure 2 shows that the proportion that watches television news is 60%. Figure 3 shows that 30% get their news from the radio.

The problem here lies with the conjunction *whereas*. It introduces a 'subordinate clause', which should be attached to a 'main clause'. In this example the subordinate *whereas* clause stands alone; it needs to be attached either to the preceding or to the following sentence, so that it is clear which contrast is being drawn, between newspapers and television or between television and radio. A subordinate clause may either follow its main clause – *Figure 1 shows …, whereas Figure 2 shows …* – or precede it – *Whereas Figure 2 shows …, Figure 3 shows …* .

4 This is the basic criteria by which we must judge the work.

How many criteria are being used? There is much confusion over whether *criteria* is a singular form (*The criteria is …*) or a plural form (*The criteria are …*). Many people, including most students, use it as a singular; but technically it is the plural form of *criterion*, a word taken from Greek along with its original plural *criteria*. So, the example should read either *These are the basic criteria …* or *This is the basic criterion …* . If you use *criteria* as a singular, what is its plural form? Is it *criterias*, perhaps?

5 This is a reasonable set of conclusions, however, they may be interpreted differently.

The problem here is knowing which part of the sentence *however* relates to. Does it go with the first part and so read *This is a reasonable set of conclusions, however. They may be interpreted differently*? Or does it go with the second part and so read *This is a reasonable set of conclusions. However, they may be interpreted differently*? As a general rule, *however*, as a word that joins sentences, goes towards the beginning of a sentence, either in initial position followed by a comma (*However, they may ...*) or near the beginning with a comma before and after (*They may, however, be ...*). If it is placed between propositions in a single written sentence, then it should be preceded or followed by a semicolon, depending on whether it goes with the following proposition (the more usual case) or the preceding one; for example *This is a reasonable set of conclusions; however, they may ... .*

Spelling, Punctuation and Grammar

We noted earlier that many people, when they think of correct grammar, mean primarily spelling and punctuation. We noted that spelling and punctuation are features specifically of writing, and that speech has grammatical organisation as much as writing. Nevertheless, spelling and punctuation are important for ensuring that your message is both readily comprehensible and taken seriously. Moreover, punctuation, as we saw with the earlier example containing defining and non-defining relative clauses, may serve to mark a vital grammatical distinction.

A text that is littered with incorrect spellings may not be incomprehensible, but it may give the impression of incompetence on the part of the writer. If you write *The principle reason for this ...* instead of *The principal reason ...*, or if you write *It served it's purpose ...* instead of *It served its purpose*, or *The guide lead them ...* instead of *The guide led them ...*, then your reader will probably get your meaning, but they may well be less inclined to take what you write seriously, because you haven't bothered to spell it properly.

English spelling is notoriously difficult, partly because it does not relate in a uniform way to pronunciation, but also because there are numerous pairs of homophones (words pronounced in the same way, but spelt differently and with a different meaning). The examples in the previous paragraph (*principle/principal, it's/its, lead/led*) are all of this kind. In other cases, the spelling may be just arbitrary: why do we spell *credible* with -*ible*, but *believable* with -*able*? And why do we change *y* to *i* in *trier* (*try* + *er*), but not in *dryer*; and can spell *flier* or *flyer* and *cryer* or *crier*? It is important to be aware of the vagaries and idiosyncrasies of English spelling, and to be ready to consult a dictionary when you are uncertain. There are also many useful spelling rules that can be learned, though it is not unusual, as with most rules of language, for there to be exceptions. One such rule you may have learned is the 'i before e except after c' rule, so *achieve*, but *receive*. The 'cei' part of this works well, but there are a number of words that have 'ei' after another letter, such as *seize, protein, surfeit, weird*. If you are not sure, look it up!

EXERCISE

What is the difference between: *to/too, horse/hoarse, affect/effect, preceding/proceeding, faint/feint*?
If you're not sure, look the words up in a dictionary.

Punctuation is another matter. Here, there is less that can be called correct or incorrect; it is more a matter of using punctuation to help your reader grasp your meaning most readily, without having to stop and work it out. Having said that, conventions for the use of punctuation marks do exist, and abiding by them will enhance your writing. A comma placed, in an inappropriate spot, can cause, confusion; just as a comma put in an appropriate place can, conceivably, help the sense. (Which punctuation marks help and which hinder in the previous sentence?)

We shall be looking at spelling rules and punctuation conventions in some detail in Chapter 9.

Summary: What Is Grammar, Then?

'Grammar' is a number of things:

1 Grammar is the means by which we structure the language that we speak and write.

2 Grammar is the set of rules, conventions and principles, together with their exceptions, that we have stored in our heads ('internalised') as a consequence of acquiring or learning the language.

3 Grammar is the set of descriptive statements, expressed in appropriate terminology ('codification'), and within a consistent framework (theory, or model) that we use to account for 'grammar' in senses 1 and 2.

4 A grammar is a book containing 3.

Knowledge of grammar is as vital to a writer as is knowledge of paint and brushstrokes to a painter, or musical notation and the characteristics of musical instruments to a composer.

This chapter has introduced the following grammatical terms. They are given brief definitions in the Glossary and explained more fully in the chapters indicated there.

conjunction	past tense
countable/uncountable	possessive
defining/non-defining	preposition
homophone	present participle
inflections	present tense
noun	subject—verb agreement
participle clause	subordinate clause
past participle	syntax

Some Basic Terminology

If you are going to reflect on your own writing, ask yourself questions about it, and seek to improve it, then you will need a vocabulary, a set of terms, to enable you to do that. In this chapter we are going to introduce some basic terminology of grammar, so that you will be equipped to do the necessary reflection to improve your writing.

Some of the terms may well be familiar to you; they are part of our everyday vocabulary. However, we will make them more precise and serviceable. Other terms you may have never heard before; they are from the technical terminology of linguistics. They are worth getting to know, because they will extend the range of your thinking about language.

Word

Let us start with the most familiar and obvious term, though for linguists it throws up some interesting problems of definition. The simplest definition would be:

A word is a sequence of letters separated by spaces from other words.

Certainly, this is how a word processing program on a computer counts words, and it is usually how you count words for a 'word limit' in an assignment. Note that this defines 'word' only in writing, not in speech; and consider the following:

1 How are *talk, talks, talking, talked* related?

2 Is *put up with* the same as *tolerate*?

3 Are *lead* (a metal) and *lead* (go ahead of) the same word?

4 Is *seat belt* one word or two?

As you have thought about these questions, it may have dawned on you that we use the term 'word' in a number of ways, to refer to different but related concepts. For example, you will find only one of the words in 1 entered in a dictionary: *talk*. This is the base form of the word; the others are 'inflected' forms. The inflections are *-s*, *-ing*, *-ed*, added to the base form. They are common to nearly all verbs in English:

-s   'third person singular present tense' inflection, used when the subject (see Chapter 4) is the equivalent of *he, she, it* (for example, 'He talks in his sleep', 'The computer talks to you')

-ing 'present participle' inflection, used to form certain verb tenses and on its own in present participle clauses (see Chapter 4) (for example, 'They are talking about the film', 'Talking of which ...')

-ed   'past tense' and 'past participle' inflection, used to form verb tenses (for example, 'They talked all night', 'I haven't talked to her since').

In terms of words on the page, *put up with* (in 2) consists of three words, but in terms of meaning it is the equivalent of *tolerate*, and like *tolerate* it would be entered as a headword in a dictionary. Items like *put up with* are called 'phrasal verbs', because they operate like a single-word verb, but they are a 'phrase' composed of a verb word (*put*) together with one or two adverbs or prepositions (see below). Phrasal verbs are usually used in informal writing and usually have a more formal single-word equivalent. Here are a few more phrasal verbs, from the hundreds in English, with their formal equivalents:

break off	**discontinue**
call out	**summon**
look down on	**despise**
speed up	**accelerate**
stand down	**resign**
take (someone) off	**imitate**

In 3, *lead* and *lead* are the same word as far as spelling is concerned, though they have a different pronunciation, and a very different meaning. They are called 'homographs' (*homo* = 'same', *graph* = 'writing'). A similar problem is presented in writing by 'homonyms', which are both spelled and pronounced the same, but have a different meaning and origin, for example, *ear* ('organ of hearing' and 'part of cereal crop' (*ear of wheat*)), *strip* ('remove one's clothing' and 'narrow piece of cloth etc.').

The example in 4 is rather like the phrasal verb in 2, in that *seat belt* consists of two written words, but has a single meaning. It is a 'compound word', but one that is written 'open', as against 'solid' (for example, *seaweed*) or 'hyphenated' (for example, *see-through*).

We can use the term 'word' quite loosely in any of the senses we have just discussed, but a more precise term may be needed where it is necessary to be more specific.

Word Classes

Before we leave words, let us note that the word stock of a language, its vocabulary or lexicon, is divided into a number of classes, based on how words are used in grammar. The traditional term for word classes is 'parts of speech', which may be a term more familiar to you.

Linguists divide the words of English into eight classes, four large ones and four relatively small ones, as follows:

noun	**pronoun**
verb	**determiner**
adjective	**preposition**
adverb	**conjunction**

Those on the left are the large classes, and the words in these classes provide most of the meaning of sentences. Those on the right are the small classes, and the words in them have a mostly supporting function in the construction of sentences.

- Nouns denote: 'things', including people (*aunt*), animals (*badger*), objects (*clock*), abstract ideas (*socialism*), feelings (*compassion*), and so on.

- Verbs denote: actions (*kick, shout*), events (*fall, lose*), states (*contain, comprise*).

- Adjectives denote: size (*large*), colour (*yellow*), shape (*oblong*), appearance (*pretty*), evaluation (*commendable*), and so on.

- Adverbs denote: manner (*cautiously*), time (*soon*), direction (*along*), etc.

- Pronouns mainly substitute for nouns and include: the personal pronouns (*I, me, mine*), reflexive pronouns (*myself, ourselves*), indefinite pronouns (*everybody, nothing*), relative pronouns (*who, whose, which*).

- Determiners accompany nouns and include: the articles (*a, the*), demonstrative determiners (*this, that*), possessive determiners (*my, our*), numerals (*five, fifth*), indefinite quantifiers (*some, few, a lot of*).

- Prepositions relate a noun to other parts of a sentence, for example, *in* the garden, *under* the sofa, *after* the lecture, *because of* the delay, *during* the night.

- Conjunctions join elements, mainly clauses, together in a sentence; they include: *and, or, but; while, whereas, although, if, that, when, so that, because*.

Some words belong to more than one word class. For example, *round* is a:

> noun in 'She bought a *round* of drinks'
> verb in 'They *round*ed the corner'
> adjective in 'Bring me a *round* dish'
> adverb in 'Come *round* tomorrow'
> preposition in 'We took a trip *round* the harbour'.

It is useful to be able to name the class that a word belongs to when talking about the structure of a sentence. Each word class is defined briefly in the Glossary at the end of the book, and dictionaries give the word class of each word entered.

EXERCISE

Word classes

To help you remember, give a word class label to each of the words in the following:

> 'Slugabed' is the perfect description for someone too lazy, too slothful, too sluggardly to drag themselves out of bed. The word was probably coined by Shakespeare and used in *Romeo and Juliet*. In Act IV, Scene V, the nurse comes to wake Juliet from her 'unnatural sleep' and says: 'Why lamb! why lady! fie, you slugabed!' At least Juliet had an excuse!

The solution is at the end of the chapter.

Sentence

The second of our terms is also familiar from the vocabulary of everyday life. Again, we have a fairly clear idea of what constitutes a sentence: a sequence of words, beginning with a capital letter and ending with a full stop, question mark or exclamation mark. This definition, like the one for word, derives from our experience of writing and does not apply in speech, which doesn't have capital letters or full stops.

If you want to reflect on what you are writing, it is more useful to think of sentences in terms of their structure. What does a sentence consist of? Looking at sentences from a structural point of view shows more clearly the choices that face the writer, and that a writer can manipulate to advantage. Some of these issues we shall elaborate on in subsequent chapters. There are a number of ways in which to approach this question. I find the following one of the most helpful and accessible.

The central, pivotal element in a sentence is the (main) verb. It is always represented by the last verb in a verb phrase (explained below); for example, in all the following verb phrases the main verb is *show*:

showed
was showing
had shown

may have shown
could be showing
must have been shown.

The choice of a verb opens up a number of other possible 'slots' in a sentence. The choice of the verb *show*, for example, would lead you to expect: 'someone' who shows, 'something' that is shown, and possibly 'someone' to whom the 'something' is shown, as in:

(The jeweller) showed (the diamond rings) (to the couple).
(You) should show (the teacher) (some respect).

Note the alternative positions for the 'something' and 'to someone' elements.

The choice of the verb *contain* expects a 'something' that is a container, and a 'something' that is the contents, for example:

(This box) contains (a first-aid kit).
(This first-aid kit) contains (all that you need to help someone in trouble).

The choice of the verb *laugh* expects a slot only for the 'someone' who laughs:

(Marley) laughed.
(All the people in the audience) were laughing.

In addition to the verb, a sentence may contain between one and three slots filled by people and things involved in the scenario that the verb is about. What can then be added to this are further elements expressing the circumstances (when, where, how, why, etc.) under which the scenario took place:

The jeweller showed the diamond rings to the couple yesterday afternoon (when?) in their own home (where?).
This box contains a first-aid kit, so that you can help anyone in need (why?).
Marley laughed uncontrollably (how?) the whole day (when?).

From this you can see that your choice of verb for a sentence will determine to a large extent its structure, what elements it will contain, and the order in which they will occur. Compare the verbs *own* and *belong to*: both expect 'something' owned and 'someone' who owns, but the order of the elements differs depending on which verb is chosen:

(Lydia) owns (the yellow car).
(The yellow car) belongs to (Lydia).

EXERCISE

What 'slots' do the following verbs open up? What kinds of element do they expect in a sentence?

come, eat, inform, tempt, yawn

Think about it, before you look at the discussion that follows.

Like many verbs of 'motion', *come* opens up two slots: one for the person(s) or vehicle that *comes*, and one for the place from which or to which they *come*. Similarly, *eat* requires a person or animal, usually, that *eats* and something, usually food, that is *eaten*. The verb *inform*, as a verb of 'communication', opens up three slots: a person *informs* another *of/about* something. *Tempt* also opens up three slots: the tempter, the person *tempted*, and the act which they are *tempted* to do. Lastly, *yawn* opens up only one slot, the person who *yawns*.

Clause

With this third main term we probably begin to enter the territory of the unknown for many of you, or the notions at least begin to get hazy. In particular, you are likely to be uncertain about the difference between 'sentence' and 'clause', and not without reason. What was said about the structure of sentences in the previous section applies equally to clauses. They, too, can be regarded as having a structure centred on a main verb. It is, thus, a defining criterion of both sentences and clauses that they contain a main verb, which determines to an extent what other elements may occur in the clause or sentence.

The difference between clauses and sentences is one of composition. Sentences may be composed of more than one clause. If a sentence contains more than one clause, they are often joined by a conjunction; for example:

(The leaves are falling from the trees), and (the days are getting shorter).
(The train arrived on time), although (it was held up near Banbury).
(I am not going out), if (I cannot afford it).
(The club has closed its doors) and (they are turning people away), because (it is already full to capacity).
When (the telephone rings) (you must answer it).

The relationships between clauses in sentences are further explored in Chapter 4.

Phrase

We tend to use the term 'phrase' in ordinary language in a rather loose sense to refer to any sequence of two or more words that go together. Linguists are rather more precise in their use of this term, and it is used to refer to particular combinations of words. Specifically, the elements filling the slots in the examples in the 'Sentence' section above correspond to what linguists mean by phrases:

the jeweller
the diamond rings
all the people in the audience
in their own home
should show
were laughing

as well as:

you
Lydia
laughed.

Phrases are the elements that fill the slots in sentence (or clause) structure, whether the element consists of one word or more than one word.

Linguists identify five types of phrase in English, each one with its own distinctive structure and based on a particular word class:

- verb phrase
- noun phrase
- adjective phrase
- adverb phrase
- prepositional phrase

VERB PHRASE (VP)

The minimal form of a verb phrase is a main verb, in one of its inflectional forms: *decide, decides, decided, deciding, to decide*. A verb phrase may additionally contain, before the main verb, a number of 'auxiliary' verbs, which contribute meanings mainly associated with time, for example:

> *are deciding*
> *was decided*
> *had decided*
> *did decide*
> *might decide*.

More than one auxiliary verb may occur in a verb phrase, and so may a negative word, especially *not*, which normally follows the first auxiliary:

> *is being decided*
> *have been deciding*
> *has not been decided*
> *might not be decided*.

A sentence or main clause must normally contain a 'finite' verb phrase, which is a verb phrase that begins with a verb that is identifiable as either 'present' or 'past' tense. All the verb phrases listed above are finite: *are, is, have, has* are present tense forms; *was, had, did, might* are past tense forms. The simple forms *decide, decides* (present) and *decided* (past) may also be finite, depending on context. The following are sentences/clauses with finite verb phrases:

The government	has decided	that taxes should be raised.
The winner	will be decided	in the morning.
The jury	decided	that the defendant was guilty.

Non-finite verb phrases consist of, or begin with, an infinitive (*to decide*) or a participle (*deciding, decided*) form of the verb. The following clauses contain non-finite verb phrases:

	Deciding	whether to go or not ...
... (difficult)	to decide	on the right verdict
	Having decided	to apply for the job ...

The incompleteness symbol (...) shows that these clauses would be part of a larger structure, for example, a sentence.

NOUN PHRASE (NP)

The minimal form of a noun phrase is a noun or pronoun: *fish, chips, decision, they, someone*. A noun phrase may additionally contain before the noun:

- **a determiner (*the, a, my, many, five*):**

  the fish
  many chips
  this decision

- **an adjective:**

	funny	fish
many	home-made	chips
this	strange	decision

- **a noun modifier:**

	river	fish
many	oven	chips
this	committee	decision

and after the noun:

- **a prepositional phrase:**

the	fish	in the sea
many	chips	from the fish-shop
this	decision	on the new road

- **a relative clause:**

the	fish	which were swimming in the sea
many	chips	that I have eaten
my	aunty	who lives in Grimsby

- **a non-finite (participle or infinitive) clause:**

the		fish	floating in the pond
many		chips	cooked by fish-shops
the	first	decision	to increase taxes.

As you can probably conclude from this small set of examples, the range and complexity of noun phrases are extensive. Here are some further examples (taken from a newspaper):

a gloomier economic outlook
Britain's most punctual inter-city train operator
the latest news from the world of personal finance
the racist police officers exposed in an undercover television programme
the Information Commissioner, who is responsible for the implementation of the Data Protection Act
a former Walt Disney executive who was responsible for marketing the Mighty Ducks ice hockey team.

ADJECTIVE PHRASE (AdjP)

The minimal form of an adjective phrase is an adjective: *funny, enormous, special, friendly, beautiful*. The adjective may be preceded by an adverb, which is usually an 'intensifier':

very funny, absolutely enormous, quite special, unusually friendly, extremely beautiful.

Some adjectives may be followed by a prepositional phrase, a *that* clause, or an infinitive clause:

satisfied with the service
sorry that I shall not be able to be with you
afraid to go out in the dark.

ADVERB PHRASE (AdvP)

The minimal form of an adverb phrase is an adverb: *sadly, eventually, soon, carelessly, afterwards, clockwise.* Some adverbs may be preceded by an 'intensifying' adverb:

very sadly
quite soon
extremely carelessly.

PREPOSITIONAL PHRASE (PrepP)

A prepositional phrase is composed of a preposition followed by a noun phrase:

on the top shelf
outside the window
before this last performance
with five bags of shopping
in spite of the bad weather.

PHRASES IN CLAUSES/SENTENCES

As noted earlier, phrases fill the slots in clause/sentence structure:

Einstein (NP) had propounded (VP) the theory of relativity (NP).
The film producer (NP) thought (VP) her (NP) very talented (AdjP).

The celebrity chef (NP) was pouring (VP) the brown liquid (NP) very carefully (AdvP) into the saucepan (PrepP).

The driver (NP) must have braked (VP) suddenly (AdvP) [and] the coach (NP) skidded (VP) on the ice (PrepP).

You (NP) look (VP) extremely smart (AdjP) in your new outfit (PrepP).

EXERCISE

Phrases

Now do the same for the following sentences:

1 Her companion was telling her a boring joke.
2 The astonished guest dropped his knife and fork with a great clatter.
3 You must climb over the garden wall immediately and escape.
4 My dear wife seems rather listless this morning.
5 You should not believe everything you read in the papers.

The solution is at the end of the chapter.

Text and Discourse

EXERCISE

Write down what you think the difference is between 'text' and 'discourse', and then read on.

These terms are both part of everyday vocabulary. A 'text' is usually taken to refer to any complete written piece of communication. It might be as short as a notice, 'Beware of the bull!', or it may be a 150,000 word novel or philosophical treatise. A 'discourse' usually refers to a piece of spoken communication, either by one person (a monologue) or by two or more (a dialogue). Some linguists have used the terms interchangeably and referred to 'spoken text' and 'written text', or to 'spoken discourse' and 'written discourse'. Since there are two terms, and they make a useful distinction, it would seem sensible to restrict 'text' to written and 'discourse' to spoken pieces of communication.

Texts may be composed of chapters, chapters of paragraphs, paragraphs of sentences. The composition will depend on how large the text is, what its purpose and readership are, and how the writer wishes to structure it. The composition of discourse is not so easily delineated. A monologue may have much the same structure as a written text, and they are very often 'written to be spoken' (e.g. a radio talk, a speech, a lecture). A dialogue involves 'turns' and sequences of turns that make up 'topics'. In this book, we are mostly concerned with written language, so the grammar of texts.

Summary

This concludes our review of some of the terminology needed for talking about grammar. In summary, we have mentioned the following, in order of 'size':

text/discourse
paragraph
sentence
clause
phrase (verb phrase, noun phrase, adjective phrase, adverb phrase, prepositional phrase)
word (noun, verb, adjective, adverb; pronoun, determiner, preposition, conjunction)

We shall be using these terms in the following chapters. They are all entered in the Glossary at the end of the book, should you need to refresh your memory about their meaning and use.

SOLUTIONS TO EXERCISES

Word classes

'Slugabed' (noun) is (verb) the (determiner) perfect (adjective) description (noun) for (preposition) someone (pronoun) too (adverb) lazy (adjective), too (adverb) slothful (adjective), too (adverb) sluggardly (adverb) to drag (verb) themselves (pronoun) out of (preposition) bed (noun). The (determiner) word (noun) was (verb) probably (adjective) coined (verb) by (preposition) Shakespeare (noun) and (conjunction) used (verb) in (preposition) *Romeo* (noun) *and* (conjunction) *Juliet* (noun). In (preposition) Act (noun) IV (number), Scene (noun) V (number), the (determiner) nurse (noun) comes (verb) to wake (verb) Juliet (noun) from (preposition) her (determiner) 'unnatural (adjective) sleep (noun)' and (conjunction) says (verb): 'Why (adverb) lamb (noun)! why (adverb) lady (noun)! fie (adverb), you (pronoun) slugabed (noun)!' At least (adverb) Juliet (noun) had (verb) an (determiner) excuse (noun)!

Phrases

1 Her companion (NP) was telling (VP) her (NP) a boring joke (NP).
2 The astonished guest (NP) dropped (VP) his knife and fork (NP) with a great clatter (PrepP).
3 You (NP) must climb (VP) over the garden wall (PrepP) immediately (AdvP) [and] escape (VP).
4 My dear wife (NP) seems (VP) rather listless (AdjP) this morning (NP).
5 You (NP) should not believe (VP) everything you read in the papers (NP).

Matching the Bits

When you sit down to write a text, you may have the impression that you are faced with unlimited choice. There are, of course, the constraints imposed by the topic you are writing on, or the question that you are supposed to be answering; but that is more likely to constrain your choice of vocabulary, rather than your choice of grammar. There is also the constraint associated with the type of text that you are writing: an essay has an expected structure, consisting of an introduction, a series of statements or arguments supported with evidence, and a conclusion. As you organise your text into a coherent sequence of paragraphs, further constraints come into play, relevant to the need to connect the paragraphs together, so that they flow. Then you will have to take account of the internal structure of paragraphs: an opening sentence that is elaborated on by subsequent sentences, and rounded off with a concluding sentence. Within each paragraph, the sentences will need to show some connection, not only by relating to a common topic, but also structurally, so that the reader is led through the developing argument or story. The right choice of words – matching verbs with suitable nouns, subjects with suitable objects – is important for making a text read fluently. The choice of one verb rather than another may influence how the reader experiences your text; a verb can change the perspective. We shall pursue some of these points further in this chapter and in subsequent chapters (see, especially, Chapters 5 and 6).

Structural choices are therefore important, because a grammatically well-crafted text will not only be more effective as a piece of communication, but also be a pleasure to read. Grammatical choices affect the meaning of the text.

EXERCISE

Compare the following sentences. How do they differ in meaning, perhaps quite subtly?

1 The appointments committee invited the distinguished scholar from Botswana to take up the post of Professor of Anthropology.
2 The distinguished scholar from Botswana was invited by the appointments committee to take up the post of Professor of Anthropology.
3 The distinguished scholar from Botswana was invited to take up the post of Professor of Anthropology by the appointments committee.
4 The distinguished scholar from Botswana was invited to take up the post of Professor of Anthropology.

The first of these sentences is 'active', the others are 'passive' in structure. The structural differences are:

- In the form of the verb phrase: passive sentences have a passive verb phrase, comprising a form of the auxiliary verb *be* (in this case *was*) + the past participle form of the main verb (in this case *invited*).

- In the order of the elements making up the sentence: in the active sentence the 'doer' (*the appointments committee*) precedes the 'action' (*invited*) as subject of the verb, and the 'victim' (*the distinguished scholar from Botswana*) follows, as object of the verb; in the passive sentence the order is reversed (the object in the active sentence becomes the subject in the passive), and the 'doer' is introduced by the preposition *by*.

Sentences 2 to 4 illustrate the variations in the ordering of elements that are possible with the passive version of the sentence, including in 4 the omission of the 'doer'. Although it could be argued that the basic propositional meaning is the same in all four sentences, the communicative meaning is different: which elements occur in initial and final positions in a sentence have a crucial effect on how a sentence is understood. The initial position is taken by what the sentence is about ('the appointments committee' or 'the distinguished scholar'); the final position is for the most 'newsworthy' item in the sentence. We shall consider the communicative effects of sentence arrangements in more detail in Chapter 5.

What Do We Talk About?

Let me suggest to you that there are three basic kinds of situation that we encode in sentences:

1 what people (mainly) *do*

2 what *happens*

3 the way things *are*.

We'll call 1 *actions*, 2 *events*, and 3 *states*. Here are some examples:

1 (a) The fire fighter took off his helmet.

 (b) They have insulted the memory of a great leader.

 (c) She considered the choices facing her.

2 (a) The glass just slipped out of my hands.

 (b) You are growing tall.

 (c) I've forgotten to buy the sprouts.

3 (a) The water is cloudy.

 (b) The baby has beautiful eyes.

 (c) We believe you are innocent.

- Actions involve a 'doer', someone (usually a person) who instigates the action: *the fire fighter* in 1a, *they* in 1b, and *she* in 1c. Actions may be physical (1a), verbal (1b), or mental (1c).

- Events encompass things that happen, but without an explicit 'doer' or instigator; they may happen to something (2a) or to someone

(2b, 2c). Events may refer to physical processes (2a, 2b), or to mental processes (2c).

- States may refer to a 'be' relationship (3a) or to a 'have' relation-ship (3b), or to a 'private state' of thinking or feeling (*believe* in 3c).

The crucial element that determines whether a sentence refers to an action, an event or a state is the main verb. In the examples above, *take off*, *insult* and *consider* are action verbs; *slip, grow* and *forget* are event verbs; and *be*, *have* and *believe* are state verbs. As we indicated in Chapter 2, the choice of main verb in a sentence or clause determines which other elements are also likely to occur. Moreover, the choice of verb can influence the perspective from which a situation is viewed. Compare:

1 The fire fighter took off his helmet (action).

2 The fire fighter's helmet has come off (event).

3 The fire fighter has no helmet on (state).

Whether we choose to report a situation as action, event or state gives an indication of how we wish a reader or hearer to view a particular state of affairs.

Choosing Your Verb

Let us pursue this line of thinking a little further by illustrating the grammatical consequences of the choice of a number of different kinds of verb. Let us begin with the verb *break*. Like a number of verbs in English, *break* may express:

- An action: *Jenny has broken your favourite mug.*

- An event: *Your favourite mug has broken.*

The action version could also be expressed in the passive, with or without the perpetrator: *Your favourite mug has been broken (by Jenny)*. As an action verb, *break* expects two participants in the sentence, the 'doer' and the 'victim'; as an event verb, it expects only one, the 'victim'.

Now consider the verbs *buy* and *sell*, which are both action verbs expecting the same three participants in the sentence: the 'seller', the 'purchaser' and the 'goods' that exchange hands. Compare:

1 Bill bought a new computer from a friend.

2 A friend sold Bill a new computer.

The choice of *buy* or *sell* to express this transaction makes a difference in the order of the elements in the sentence, and in the perspective from which the transaction is reported. With *buy* the purchaser is the 'doer' in subject position, and the seller comes last in a prepositional phrase introduced by *from*; whereas with *sell*, the 'seller' is the initial 'doer' element, and the final position may be taken by the 'goods', as in 2 above, or by the purchaser, as in:

3 A friend sold a new computer to Bill.

Let us look next at the verb *think*. This verb is used mainly as a 'private' state, to express a belief or an opinion, and the most common 'experiencer' of the private state is 'I':

1 I think (that) the conflict will continue for some time.

2 I think Julia (to be) the best violinist in the orchestra.

These are the two main grammatical structures with *think* as a private state verb. In 1 the 'thought' is expressed by a *that* clause, although the introductory conjunction *that* is often omitted. In 2, where an opinion is being expressed about someone, there are two elements after the verb, which may be joined by *to be*. First is the person or thing about which an opinion is being expressed (*Julia*), followed by the evaluation (*the best violinist* ...). These two elements could be related in a 'be' type of state:

3 Julia is the best violinist in the orchestra.

The verb *think* may also be used to express a mental process action:

4 Boris is thinking about his next move.

Finally, let us take the verb *smell*. As an action verb, *smell* expects a 'doer', the person (or animal) that deliberately puts their nose to something:

1 **The badger smelt the food that had been put out.**

However, this sentence could refer to an involuntary smelling: the odour of the food reached the badger's nostrils. Compare:

2 **The badger could smell the food that had been put out.**

Here, with the addition of the modal auxiliary *could*, the involuntary meaning is the only one possible. Perhaps, with this meaning, *smell* expresses an event rather than an action. In a quite different structure, *smell* has a state meaning:

3 **These flowers smell rather nice.**

4 **These curtains smell of stale tobacco smoke.**

5 **You smell.**

As a state verb, *smell* can be followed either by an adjective, as in 3 (*nice*), or by a prepositional phrase introduced by *of* (4), or by nothing (5). When *smell* contains only an element referring to the thing emitting an odour, then it implies an unpleasant odour.

This selection of verbs illustrates that the choice of verb influences the structure of the sentence or clause in which it performs its pivotal role. It also shows that some verbs can enter more than one structure, sometimes with quite distinct meanings, at other times with a more nuanced difference. When you are writing, it is useful to try out the different structures that are possible with a given verb, to see which one fits best into the text that you are composing.

EXERCISE

Construct as many different sentence structures as you can with each of the following verbs. How does each structure change the perspective on what is being communicated?

close, e.g. The attendant closed the door — The door was closed — The door closed

feel

suggest

Circumstances

A main verb has some influence over the occurrence of other elements in its sentence, but that influence does not usually extend to the 'circumstance' elements. By 'circumstances', we mean the where, when, how and why of a situation. Some verbs do expect a 'where' circumstance to be present in their sentence, for example *keep* and *put*, in the structure 'someone keeps/puts something somewhere':

1 We keep the cut-glass bowls in the cabinet.

2 She put the letters into the postbox.

The verb *last* expects a 'when' circumstance of duration (how long?):

3 The performance lasts for three hours.

Such verbs are, however, in the minority; and the vast majority of verbs set up no strong expectations about the occurrence of particular circumstances in their sentences. They may be freely and optionally added.

Having said that circumstances may be freely added to any sentence, it is, nevertheless, the case that a circumstance must be compatible in meaning with the sentence to which it is added. If the sentence is in the past tense, for example, and a time circumstance is added, then this must have past time reference:

> The army fired (past tense) a missile at the compound last night (past time).

You could not say: '… next week' (future time), as it would be incompatible with the tense of the verb.

Similarly, a direction circumstance (*to* or *from* somewhere) is appropriate only with a verb that denotes movement:

> She walked/strode/crept towards the door.

Let us at this point review the main types of circumstances that we may wish to add to a sentence. Broadly, we may wish to add information about time, place, manner, reason, purpose, or condition. Time may indicate 'when' an action or event takes place, or may refer to 'how long' a situation takes or lasts, or to 'how frequently' it occurs.

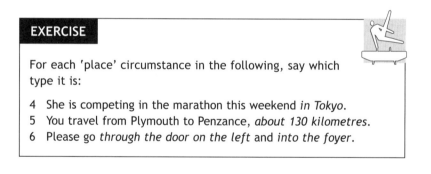

EXERCISE

For each of the following, say which type of 'time' circumstance it is:

1 She has been writing the history essay *for four days.*
2 They go to the cinema *twice a week.*
3 The first atom bomb was dropped on Hiroshima *on 6 August 1945.*

Place may indicate 'where' a situation occurs or is the case, or may refer to 'direction' (where from, to, or via), or to 'distance' (how far).

EXERCISE

For each 'place' circumstance in the following, say which type it is:

4 She is competing in the marathon this weekend *in Tokyo.*
5 You travel from Plymouth to Penzance, *about 130 kilometres.*
6 Please go *through the door on the left* and *into the foyer.*

Manner indicates 'how' an action/event occurred; reason indicates 'why' a situation occurred or exists; purpose indicates 'what for' something is done; and condition indicates 'under what condition' something occurs or exists.

EXERCISE

Which circumstance in the following indicates manner, reason, condition, purpose?

7   The redundancies were handled *rather insensitively.*
8   *If you complete this form,* we shall be able to consider your application.
9   She is running the Tokyo marathon to *raise money for charity.*
10 The game has been postponed *because of the bad weather.*

The answers are as follows: (1) how long; (2) how frequently; (3) when; (4) where; (5) distance; (6) direction; (7) manner; (8) condition; (9) purpose; (10) reason. This does not exhaust all possible circumstances, but gives an indication of the main ones. You will note that a circumstance may be expressed by:

- a prepositional phrase: *for four days, in Tokyo*

- a noun phrase: *about 130 kilometres*

- an adverbial clause: *if you complete this form.*

Summarising so far: the choice of the 'main' verb in a sentence both predicts and constrains the presence of 'obligatory' elements (subject, objects, complement). It only occasionally predicts the usually 'optional' circumstances (adverbials), but it constrains them to the extent that their meaning(s) need to be compatible.

Collocation

Compatibility of meaning extends beyond the appropriateness of an adverbial for a sentence. Other word combinations may be ineligible because they violate lexical or semantic compatibility conventions. To take a simple example, if your cup of tea has been made using a large amount of tea and left to brew for a considerable time, then you will probably have a 'strong' cup of tea. Its opposite would be 'weak' tea. There is no particular reason why we use 'strong' and 'weak' in respect of tea, rather than, say, 'dark' and 'light', or 'thick' and 'thin'. But 'strong' and 'weak' collocate with 'tea', rather than any other pair of adjectives. That is a fact about this particular micro-structure of English.

Such collocational compatibilities permeate the language, and linguists are still discovering what the conventions are in this area, and the degree of freedom that a speaker or writer has in any particular context. For example, the numeral expression 'a brace of' (meaning 'a pair of') is usually applied to two kinds of item: birds, animals and fish that are 'hunted' (*a brace of pheasant, rabbits, carp*); and firearms, especially *a brace of pistols*. However, you now find that 'a brace of' crops up in some unlikely places, such as sports reporting: *a brace of goals, tries, wickets*. But you still cannot use 'a brace of' for just any pair of things: *a brace of gloves, socks, shoes, chairs*.

Collocation operates across a number of structures, including adjective + noun, verb + object, verb + adverb. Take the adjective *heavy*, for example. Its usual meaning is concerned with 'weight'; a 'heavy' object is one that weighs a lot. But *heavy* collocates with a number of nouns where the 'weight' meaning is absent, though a transferred meaning of 'large extent' does apply:

> heavy breathing; heavy casualties; heavy cold; heavy defeat; heavy drinking; heavy fines; heavy rain; heavy schedule; heavy seas; heavy sleeper; heavy smoker; heavy use.

The use of *heavy* in these contexts is arbitrary, and a learner of English as a foreign language would not be able to guess that *heavy* would be the appropriate adjective to indicate a 'large extent' for these nouns. Such arbitrary collocations are not unusual. Consider:

> *deep* divisions; *deep* trouble; *fat* chance; *fat* profit; take *full* advantage; the *full* story; *high* opinion; *high* praise; in *poor* taste; *poor* value; *tall* order; *tall* story; *tame* excuse; *tame* joke; *wide* margin; *wide* vocabulary.

Constructing sentences also involves being aware of which adjectives can collocate with the nouns that you wish to use.

Similarly, the appropriate match of verb and object may also be a matter of collocation. For example, you 'spend' time and money, but you 'expend' energy or effort; and you can 'waste' all of them. You can 'arrive at', 'come to' or 'reach' a decision; you may then 'implement', 'overturn' or 'go back on' it. With a promise, however, you can 'make' it, 'keep' it, 'break' it, 'go back on' it or 'renege on' it. Here are some further examples of verb + object collocations:

> *break* a contract, habit, journey, record, strike
> *command* attention, respect, support, a high price
> *grant* approval, asylum, a concession, a pardon, permission
> *mount* a campaign, a challenge, an exhibition, a search
> *spoil* your appetite, your chances, the effect, the view, yourself.

Matching verbs and object nouns is clearly important for achieving a fluent text. Creative use of language, however, may involve attempting to extend the collocational range of a word.

Let us look at our third set of collocation examples: verb + adverb, such as *laugh heartily*. There is a limited number of ways in which we can describe laughing; besides 'heartily', there is 'loudly', 'hysterically', 'one's head off', and perhaps one or two more. Sometimes, the adverb is related to the adjective that is used with the related noun: *drink heavily – heavy drinker, laugh hysterically – hysterical laughter, oppose resolutely – resolute opposition*. Here are some further examples of verb + adverb collocations:

> complain, regret, resent *bitterly*
> breathe, think, regret *deeply*
> accept, agree, live, settle *happily*
> correlate, identify, respond *positively*
> applaud, greet, receive, welcome *warmly*.

If you are a speaker of English as your first language, then you may feel that your intuitions are a good guide to collocational compatibilities; and you are probably right. However, it is good to be aware of this dimension of choice, or constraint; as just occasionally our intuitions may desert us.

There is just one further, related matter to mention in connection with semantic compatibility. Think of the types of object that you would typically find following the verb *commit*. You will come up with a list that is likely to include nouns such as:

adultery, crime, error, offence, murder, rape, sin, suicide.

You will notice that all these nouns have a 'negative' meaning; and, generally speaking, it would appear that you cannot 'commit' anything very pleasant. *Commit* spreads a negative meaning; it occurs in a sentence in which the accompanying words tend to have unpleasant and negative meanings. Similarly, the verb *wreak* has a negative influence, occurring with nouns such as:

havoc, mayhem, destruction; revenge, vengeance.

Words may have positive, as well as negative, influences. For example, you can *embark on a*:

career, journey, programme, project, tour.

The adjective *warm*, similarly, has a positive meaning, occurring in phrases such as 'lovely and warm', 'warm and friendly', 'cosy and warm', 'soft and warm'.

Summary

In this chapter we have seen that, while grammar allows a measure of creativity to the writer, and the writer has to exercise choice in selecting the words, phrases and constructions that best fit the purpose of the text, there are, nevertheless, a number of constraints, both syntactic and semantic, that operate to determine the shape that a sentence, and ultimately a text, will take. Knowing about what is possible and what is constrained in grammar will make you a more self-aware writer, and therefore a more proficient one. In the following chapters, we consider in more detail how sentences may be structured and arranged to achieve optimum communicative effect.

The follow terms have featured in this chapter. You may wish to remind yourself of how they are used by looking them up in the Glossary at the end of the book.

active/passive
action   event   state
circumstance
time   place   condition
reason   purpose   manner
collocation

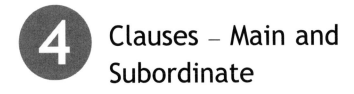

Clauses – Main and Subordinate

The nub of syntax is the structure of the clause. Choices made here have an influence on adjoining clauses and sentences, and ultimately on the way a text as a whole develops its message. In this chapter, then, we're going to look at the structure of sentences and clauses, to examine the kinds of choice that we make as writers, and to acquire some terminology for talking about this aspect of grammar. We begin by looking at the 'simple sentence', composed of one clause; and then we examine complex sentences, composed of two or more clauses.

Simple Sentence

The minimal form of a sentence is subject + verb:

1 **The gaoler + laughed.**

2 **The wind + has dropped.**

3 **The street + has been cleaned.**

The subject slot is normally filled by a noun phrase, and the verb slot by a verb phrase. Where relevant, the head noun of the subject noun phrase 'agrees in number with' the first verb of the verb phrase; compare:

3 **The street has been cleaned.**

4 **The streets have been cleaned.**

Because 'street' in 3 is singular in number, the verb is 'has', the 'third person singular present tense' form; whereas in 4 the plural 'streets' requires the plural form 'have'. This agreement rule, often cited as a marker of standard English, applies only with present tense verbs; compare:

1   The gaoler laughed.

5   The gaolers laughed.

However, there is one very common verb – *be* – where the agreement applies in both present and past tenses:

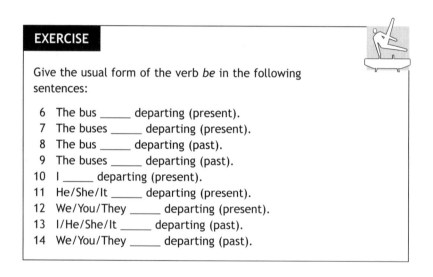

EXERCISE

Give the usual form of the verb *be* in the following sentences:

6   The bus _____ departing (present).
7   The buses _____ departing (present).
8   The bus _____ departing (past).
9   The buses _____ departing (past).
10   I _____ departing (present).
11   He/She/It _____ departing (present).
12   We/You/They _____ departing (present).
13   I/He/She/It _____ departing (past).
14   We/You/They _____ departing (past).

The accepted written forms are: (6) is, (7) are, (8) was, (9) were, (10) am, (11) is, (12) are, (13) was, (14) were. In colloquial speech, some people use *was* for both singular and plural past:

15   We/You/They was departing.

All the examples of subject + verb sentences above follow the normal order for 'statements', which will be taken as the basic order: subject before verb.

Three further types of elements may occur in simple sentences, normally after the verb. They will in part be determined by the main verb in the sentence (see Chapter 3). A simple sentence may, in addition to the subject + verb, contain an object slot:

1   The strikers + welcomed + the decision.

2   The caretaker + has replaced + the light bulb.

3   Spiders + have + eight legs.

Where the subject denotes a 'doer', the object usually represents the 'victim', the entity having something done to them (as in 1 and 2). In a 'have'-type state (3), the 'possessor' is subject and the 'entity possessed' is object. With some verbs (for example, *giving* and *telling*), a second object may occur:

4   The salesman + offered + the enquirers + a bargain.

5   The explorer + related + his adventures + to the audience.

In these cases we talk of a 'direct object', which is the entity most immediately affected by the action, so the 'victim': *a bargain* in 4 and *his adventures* in 5. The other object is called an 'indirect object', and it usually refers to a recipient or beneficiary of the action: *the enquirers* in 4 and *the audience* in 5. An indirect object does not normally occur unless a direct object is also present in the sentence; it usually refers to a person or other animate being, or some entity associated with people, such as an organisation. It is expressed either by a noun phrase, when it precedes the direct object, as in 4, or by a prepositional phrase, usually introduced by *to* or *for*, when it follows the direct object, as in 5.

The second kind of element that follows the verb in a simple sentence is the complement, as in:

1   Lydia + is + a mathematician.

2   Lydia + seems + very intelligent.

3   They + have appointed + Jane + as the department's representative.

4   Nobody + considers + the law + effective.

The last element in each case is the complement. In the first two examples, it is a subject complement, in the last two an object complement. The complement reflects back on and 'complements' the subject or object; it is in some way descriptive of the other element. So, *mathematician* and *very intelligent* complement *Lydia*; *the department's representative* complements *Jane*; and *effective* complements *the law*. The complement slot is filled by either an adjective phrase (*very intelligent, effective*), or a noun phrase (*a mathematician*), or a prepositional phrase (*as the department's representative*). Complements occur after only a fairly restricted set of verbs: *be, seem, appear* and similar verbs take subject complements; and *consider, judge, think* and similar verbs, along with *appoint, vote* and the like, take object complements. Some object complements may be preceded by a preposition like *as* (3 above), or by *to be*, as in:

5 Nobody considers the law to be effective.

The third kind of element to follow the verb in simple sentences is the adverbial. An adverbial, of which there may be more than one in a sentence, refers to a range of 'circumstances' surrounding an action, event or state (see Chapter 3). Such circumstances may relate to place – where something is or has happened, or to or from where someone goes or comes:

1 The town of Ross + stands + above the Wye Valley.

2 An important Civil War battle + took place + near Worcester.

3 You + put + the dish + into the oven.

4 They + haven't returned + from holiday in France.

Some verbs expect a place adverbial to be present (*put* in 3 and *return* in 4), while in most cases the addition of information about place is entirely optional. Where an adverbial is optional, its position in the sentence may be variable:

5 Above the Wye Valley stands the town of Ross.

6 Near Worcester an important Civil War battle took place.

An adverbial may relate to time – when something happened, how long something took, how often something occurred:

1 I + received + the letter from the university + on Tuesday.

2 We + stayed + in Paris + (for) two weeks.

3 You + must change + the dressing + daily/every day.

Time adverbials may be expressed by an adverb (*daily*), or by a noun phrase (*two weeks, every day*), or most often by a prepositional phrase (*on Tuesday, for two weeks*).

An adverbial may relate to how something happened, which includes the manner in which something was done, as well as the means or instrument used:

1   You + must remove + the glass plate + very carefully.

2   We + go + to the library + by bus.

3   You + can adjust + the mechanism + with a screwdriver.

Basic manner adverbials are expressed by means of manner adverbs, which are usually derived from adjectives with the *-ly* suffix (*careful-ly, nervous-ly*). Means is normally expressed by a prepositional phrase introduced by *by* (*by bus, by (means of) filtration*); but note *on foot*. Instruments are also normally expressed by a prepositional phrase introduced by *with* (*with a screwdriver*).

An adverbial may relate to why something happened (reason), to what end it happened (purpose), or under what condition it happened:

1   The plan + failed + because of his incompetence.

2   They + are building + a new road + to relieve congestion.

3   If you wish to claim + you + must supply + evidence of your circumstances.

The reason adverbial in 1 is a prepositional phrase, introduced by *because of*; it could equally as well have been a clause introduced by *because*:

4   The plan + failed + because he was incompetent.

The other two adverbials, in 2 and 3, are expressed by clauses. The purpose adverbial is a *to* infinitive clause (*to relieve congestion*); alternatively, but less often, it may be a *for* prepositional phrase:

5   They + did + it + for a laugh.

The condition adverbial is an *if* clause, which expresses the condition under which something happens or may happen. Condition adverbials frequently take initial position in a sentence.

With this last set of adverbials, we have strayed beyond the limits of the simple sentence into those that are composed of more than one clause, on which more below. Before that, let us summarise the structure of a simple sentence. The minimal sentence is composed of:

subject + verb (*Emma + smiled*)

A sentence may additionally contain one or two objects:

subject + verb + object (*Emma + consulted + her diary*)
subject + verb + indirect object + direct object (*Emma + offered + Francis + an alternative date*)

A sentence may alternatively contain a complement, either of the subject or of the object:

subject + verb + complement (*Emma + is + a shrewd woman*)
subject + verb + object + complement (*Emma + considers + Francis' behaviour + unethical*)

A sentence may contain a more-or-less obligatory adverbial, usually of place:

subject + verb + adverbial (*Emma + is travelling + to Russia*)
subject + verb + object + adverbial (*Emma + threw + her diary + at Francis*)

These are the basic structures, the models for all simple sentences. Additionally, a sentence may optionally contain one or more adverbials of place, time, manner, reason, etc.

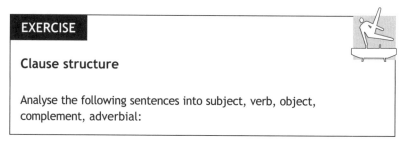

EXERCISE

Clause structure

Analyse the following sentences into subject, verb, object, complement, adverbial:

---

1   The Loire valley – is – one of France's most beautiful regions.
2   This trip – will give – you – a good introduction to the region.
3   A coach – will take – you – to Monet's house and garden.
4   People – regard – Chartres Cathedral – as the most magnificent in France.
5   This evening – we – eat – in a charming restaurant.

The solution is at the end of the chapter.

Compound Sentence

When two or more simple sentences are joined together by means of a co-ordinating conjunction (*and*, *but*, *or*), they form a 'compound' sentence, and the components are called 'clauses'. The clauses are essentially independent sentences, which could stand alone. For example:

1   **The number of homeless people has risen, and/but there is less accommodation available for them.**

2   **The number of homeless people has risen. There is less accommodation available for them.**

The conjunction (*and/but*) in the compound sentence in 1 makes the relationship between the two propositions more explicit. In a sense, it demands less work of the reader. The reader has to infer the relationship between the simple sentences in 2.

When two clauses are co-ordinated, items that are identical in both may be omitted from one of the clauses, usually the second one:

1   **The victim may have injected himself, or he may have taken sleeping pills.**

2   **The victim may have injected himself or taken sleeping pills.**

The second clause of 2 omits the subject (*the victim/he*) and the auxiliary verbs from the verb phrase (*may have*). The omitted items are 'recoverable' from the first clause, so both clauses can still be said to be potentially independent simple sentences, though the 'or' relationship probably needs to be made explicit:

3 The victim may have injected himself. Alternatively, he may have taken sleeping pills.

Without *alternatively*, the relationship could be interpreted as 'and' rather than 'or':

4 The victim may have injected himself. He may have taken sleeping pills.

Compound sentences have the advantage of enabling you to be clear about the relationship you want your reader to understand between one proposition and another that follows.

Complex Sentence

A complex sentence results from the inclusion of one sentence as an element in another. The included sentence is said to be 'embedded', and it is termed a 'subordinate clause'. The sentence into which it is embedded is called the 'main clause'. There are many kinds of subordinate or embedded clause, which we will review; but let us begin with a simple example:

1 The security forces ordered that the area should be cleared.

The clauses in this example are as follows:

main – The security forces ordered (something)
subordinate – that the area should be cleared.

The subordinate clause fills the object slot in the main clause; it is the object of *ordered*. It is a *'that* clause', introduced by the conjunction *that*. If the conjunction is removed, the clause has the full structure of a simple sentence: subject (*the area*) + verb (*should be cleared*). Not all subordinate clauses are like this:

2 **The student asked to be excused the examination.**

main – The student asked (something)
subordinate – to be excused the examination.

In this case the subordinate clause has an infinitive form of the verb (*to be excused*) followed by an object (*the examination*), but it contains no subject. It is called a '*to* infinitive clause'.

Subordinate Clauses

Subordinate clauses like the *that* clause and *to* infinitive clause above are 'noun' clauses, because they fill slots (subject and object in particular) that are usually filled by nouns or noun phrases. Other types of subordinate clause are: 'adjectival', functioning like adjectives in describing nouns; and 'adverbial', functioning like adverbs in the adverbial slot in sentence structure. We'll review each of these types of clause in turn, so that we know what we're talking about.

NOUN CLAUSES

There are four main kinds of noun clause in English: *that* clause, *wh-* clause, infinitive clause, and *-ing* clause. They can all function as either subject or object within a main clause, though it is more usual to find a noun clause as object than as subject. Here are some examples:

1 *That he was given the scholarship* suggests a corrupt system (*that* clause as subject).

2 She told us *that the museum didn't open until 10 o'clock* (*that* clause as (direct) object).

3 *What she wanted to know* was the opening times (*wh-* clause as subject).

4 The announcer explained *why the train was late* (*wh-* clause as object).

Wh- clauses are introduced by a *wh-* word (*who, what, when, where, why, how*), which is not just a conjunction, like *that* in a *that* clause, but is also an element within the *wh-* clause itself (as subject, object, complement, adverbial): *what* is object of *know* in 3, and *why* is an adverbial (of reason) within the *wh-* clause in 4. Both *that* clauses and *wh-* clauses are finite clauses with a complete sentence structure. This is not the case for infinitive clauses and *-ing* clauses, which are both non-finite clauses, usually without a subject:

5 *To* lose this match is a catastrophe (infinitive clause as subject).

6 They are always wanting *to influence the outcome* (infinitive clause as object).

7 *Discovering a new species* is rarely achieved by a botanist (*-ing* clause as subject).

8 They regretted *signing the contract* (*-ing* clause as object).

All the noun clauses in these sentences are potentially 'subject + verb + object' structures, but they do not have a subject, and the verb is non-finite (infinitive, present participle). In some cases, it is possible to include a subject with a non-finite noun clause; though, with infinitive clauses, it may be introduced by *for*:

9 *For them to lose this match* is a catastrophe.

10 They are always wanting *their stooges to influence the outcome*.

11 They regretted *Monica signing the contract*.

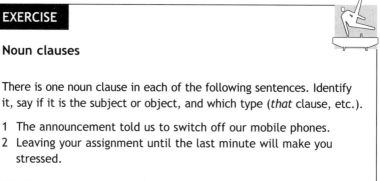

EXERCISE

Noun clauses

There is one noun clause in each of the following sentences. Identify it, say if it is the subject or object, and which type (*that* clause, etc.).

1 The announcement told us to switch off our mobile phones.
2 Leaving your assignment until the last minute will make you stressed.

3 The college has agreed that you can pay in instalments.

4 I do not know what this track is called.

5 To err is human.

The solution is at the end of the chapter.

ADJECTIVAL CLAUSES

The major function of adjectives (see Chapter 2) is within noun phrases, to add descriptive information about nouns:

a *large* house, a *successful* application, the *empty* glass, twelve *fresh-baked* loaves, the *previous urgent* request, all this *unnecessary* fuss.

Adjectival clauses have a similar function; however, because they are longer, they are positioned after the noun to which they relate. There are two basic types of adjectival clause: finite, which are called 'relative' clauses; and non-finite, which are participle clauses. Here, first, are some examples of relative clauses:

1 the large house *that/which we looked at yesterday*

2 a successful application, *which came in at the last moment*

3 the empty glass *to which I was referring*

4 my favourite aunt, *who(m) I shall visit on Thursday*

5 the scientist *who/that made this discovery*

6 the animal *whose feet made these tracks.*

Relative clauses have a similar structure to *wh-* clauses: they are introduced by a relative pronoun (*who, whom, whose, which, that*), which is an element of the relative clause: *that/which* is object of *looked* in 1, *which* is subject of *came in* in 2, *whom* is object of *visit* in 4, and *who/that* is subject of *made* in 5. In 3, *which* is preceded by the preposition *to* because the verb is *refer to*; and in 6, *whose* is equivalent of possessive *his/her/its* in *whose feet*. The object form of the *who* relative pronoun – *whom* (in 4) – is only now used in fairly formal writing. The difference between *which* and *who* is one of 'person': *who* relates to a noun referring to a person, *which* to one referring to a non-personal noun. The possessive relative pronoun *whose* belongs to the personal *who* set, but it is increasingly found with non-personal nouns:

7   the bus company whose drivers are on strike

8   the bus, whose windows needed cleaning.

The alternative to 8 would be:

9   the bus, of which the windows needed cleaning

or

10   the bus, the windows of which needed cleaning

Both of which are rather complicated by comparison with 8. Otherwise a relative clause is to be avoided:

11   the bus — its windows needed cleaning — ... .

In Chapter 1, we showed that a knowledge of relative clause structure is necessary to understand whether to put a comma before a relative pronoun. You do not put a comma if the relative clause is 'defining', when it is used to define or specify which noun is being referred to. In 1 above, for example, the relative clause (*that we looked at yesterday*) specifies which 'large house' is being talked about. Similarly in 5, *who made this discovery* specifies 'the scientist' under discussion. In fact, the use of *that* as a relative pronoun is only possible if the relative clause is defining. By contrast, *which came in at the last moment* in 2 and *whom I shall visit on Thursday* in 4 are non-defining relative clauses: they are simply adding further information about the noun.

Here are now some examples of non-finite adjectival clauses:

12   the total sum *raised so far*

13   the return to work, *negotiated by the unions yesterday*

14   the overall impression *resulting from the investigations*

15   the president, *speaking in a private capacity*.

The first two examples (12 and 13) contain a past participle introducing the adjectival clause (*raised, negotiated*), and the other two examples (14 and 15) contain a present participle (*resulting, speaking*). As with non-finite noun clauses, it is the subject that is missing. Non-finite adjectival clauses could be viewed as reduced relative clauses – a passive clause for past participles, and an active clause for present participles:

16 the total sum which/that has been raised so far

17 the return to work, which has been negotiated by the unions

18 the overall impression which/that results from the investigations

19 the president, who is/was speaking in a private capacity.

You will notice from the use or absence of a comma that non-finite adjectival clauses may be defining (12 and 14) or non-defining (13 and 15), just like relative clauses.

There is one further, but not very common non-finite adjectival clause – an infinitive clause:

20 the long-jumper *to watch this summer*

21 the most versatile computer *to appear on the market this year*.

Adjectival infinitive clauses often occur in examples like 21, where the noun is preceded by an adjective in the superlative degree (*most versatile*).

EXERCISE

Adjectival clauses

Identify the adjectival clauses in the following sentences. Say if the adjectival clause is finite (a relative clause) or non-finite (a participle or infinitive clause).

1 The hypothesis suggested by my colleague is not supported by the evidence.
2 My colleague, for whom I have the greatest respect, is mistaken.

3 A different result emerges from the experiments that I have conducted.

4 An experiment measuring the flow of water has led to a different outcome.

5 It is an outcome which has been verified by other experiments.

The solution is at the end of the chapter.

ADVERBIAL CLAUSES

With the function of adverbials in sentence structure, adverbial clauses express various types of circumstance information (see above and Chapter 3). An adverbial clause is typically a finite clause introduced by a subordinating conjunction that indicates the type of circumstance information that the clause is intended to convey:

1 *Where she had planted grass seed,* buttercups were growing (place).

2 *When the alarm sounds,* everyone must evacuate the building (time).

3 No one knows the results of the tests, *because the laboratory has suppressed them* (reason).

4 *If you take that road,* you will have to pay a toll (condition).

5 *Although we didn't reach the summit,* we enjoyed the walk up the hill (concession).

6 You must arrange the matchsticks *so that they form a hexagon* (result).

We have illustrated only one adverbial clause of time in this set of examples, but the time relationships between actions and events are often expressed in this way, by subordinating conjunctions like *before, after, while, since, until.*

There is one type of circumstance meaning that is expressed not by an adverbial clause but by an infinitive clause, and that is 'purpose':

7 **We are going to the bank** *to change some currency.*

8 *To access the service,* **you must type in your PIN number.**

Why Use Compound and Complex Sentences?

If we were to speak or write in a series of simple sentences, it would make for rather uninteresting discourse. Moreover, we would be unable to express the complexity of thought that a more complex grammar enables us to do. In our thinking we make connections between things, which then need to find expression in the grammar of what we say or write.

If we are reporting what someone said or wrote, then what we report will be a proposition, a sentence in itself. So, it is inevitably the case that verbs of reporting (*say, tell, report, comment,* etc.) will have a subordinate clause as object containing the proposition.

If we are telling a story and putting events into a narrative sequence, then it is highly likely that we will want to relate events to each other explicitly in time, by a number of means, including adverbial clauses of time.

If we are constructing an argument, then we will need to relate contrasting theses, adduce conflicting evidence, draw alternative conclusions. The grammar of complex sentences enables us to do that.

If we are explaining how something works, or the rules of a game, or the reasons for some course of action, then we shall need to make connections between part and whole, cause and effect, state of affairs and reasons for it.

Complex communication requires complex grammar. Knowing what grammatical resources are available to you, being able to make judicious choices from among them, will make you a more reflective and skilful communicator, especially in writing.

EXERCISE

Subordinate clauses

Which are the subordinate clauses in the following sentences? For each one, say whether it is a noun, an adjectival, or an adverbial clause.

1 People who live on the estate were feeling isolated.
2 Now they are celebrating because their hard work has been recognised.
3 What impressed me was that residents of all ages got stuck in.
4 She decided to set up a residents' group to tap into the funds.
5 Getting all ages involved has created a sense of local identity.
6 When they see people making an effort, kids won't be antisocial.
7 This is an example of a small investment that can have a big effect.
8 We placed bollards at the end so that kids who had nicked cars couldn't get on the estate.
9 If you break the problem down and do small things, it can start the ball rolling.
10 This shows that a small investment can have a big effect.

The solution is at the end of the chapter.

Summary

This chapter has introduced quite a number of grammatical terms. The following are the main ones. They are all in the Glossary at the end of the book. If you are not sure how they are used, look them up in the Glossary, or revise the relevant section of this chapter.

clause
simple sentence   compound sentence   complex sentence
subject   verb   object   complement   adverbial
direct object   indirect object

subordinate clause   embedded clause
noun clause   adjectival clause   adverbial clause
that clause   *wh-* clause   *-ing* clause
infinitive clause
relative clause   participle clause

SOLUTIONS TO EXERCISES

Clause structure

1 subject — verb — complement
2 subject — verb — indirect object — direct object
3 subject — verb — object — adverbial
4 subject — verb — object — complement
5 adverbial — subject — verb — adverbial.

Noun clauses

1 to switch off our mobile phones: object, infinitive clause
2 leaving your assignment until the last minute: subject, *-ing* clause
3 that you can pay in instalments: object, *that* clause
4 what this track is called: object, *wh-* clause
5 to err: subject, infinitive clause.

Adjectival clauses

1 suggested by my colleague: participle clause (non-finite)
2 for whom I have the greatest respect: relative clause (finite)
3 that I have conducted: relative clause (finite)
4 measuring the flow of water: participle clause (non-finite)
5 which has been verified by other experiments: relative clause (finite).

Subordinate clauses

1 who live on the estate: adjectival, relative clause
2 because their hard work has been recognised: adverbial clause of reason
3 what impressed me: noun, *wh-* clause (subject)

   that residents of all ages got stuck in: noun, *that* clause (object)

4 to set up a residents' group: noun, infinitive clause (object)

   to tap into the funds: adverbial, infinitive clause of purpose

5 getting all ages involved: noun, *-ing* clause (subject)
6 when they see people making an effort: adverbial clause of time

   people making an effort: noun, *-ing* clause (object of 'see')

7 that can have a big effect: adjectival, relative clause
8 so that kids who had nicked cars couldn't get on the estate: adverbial clause of purpose

   who had nicked cars: adjectival, relative clause

9 if you break the problem down and do small things: adverbial clause of condition

   the ball rolling: noun, *-ing* clause (object of 'start')

10 that a small investment can have a big effect: noun, *that* clause (object).

5 Sentence Arrangements

When we put sentences together into a paragraph or text, we need to pay particular attention to the choice of elements to fill the initial and final slots of the sentence. These positions in sentence structure have a particular significance in the developing communication of a text. What a sentence starts with usually relates back in some way to the previous sentence or sentences in the text, and it thus serves to tie the present sentence into the text structure. It also represents the 'theme' or starting point of the sentence, what the sentence is about. The final position in a sentence usually contains the most 'newsworthy' element, and it thus contributes to carrying forward the message of the text. Consideration of how you distribute material within a sentence can contribute to success in getting your point across.

Rearrangement

EXERCISE

Rewrite the following sentence, bringing in turn as many of the elements as possible into initial position.

They have offered the manager's job to Barry.

As it stands, with the third person pronoun *they* as the first element, the reference of *they* must be looked for in a previous sentence. Presumably, it stands for a noun such as 'interview panel' or 'board', which has already been mentioned; and so *they* provides a link from this sentence back into the text. The final, most newsworthy, element in this sentence is 'to Barry': it is saying that the offer of the job to Barry, rather than to anyone else, is the most significant piece of information. If, on the other hand, Barry was already in the frame for a job and the significant fact was which job he would be offered, then the sentence would have to read:

They have offered Barry the manager's job.

or

To Barry they have offered the manager's job.

If 'the manager's job' is what is being talked about, then it could take up first position:

The manager's job they offered to Barry.

Since the initial and final elements in sentences are so important to enabling the message of a text to be developed successfully, it is not surprising that there are grammatical processes for rearranging the order of elements in a sentence, in order to move elements to these initial and final positions. In our example sentence it is possible to reposition the elements without using any specific grammatical process:

To Barry they have offered the manager's job: implies that 'Barry' is the current topic of the text.
The manager's job they have offered to Barry: implies that 'the manager's job' is in focus at this point in the text.

The one sequence that is unalterable in this statement sentence is that of subject (*they*) + verb (*have offered*). The reason for the relative flexibility of the structure of this sentence is that it is possible to identify easily the function of the elements without relying on their syntactic position:

they has the subject form of the third person pronoun
to Barry is indirect object because it is a prepositional phrase introduced by *to*
the manager's job is, therefore, by default the direct object.

Sometimes the meaning allows identification of the functions of elements. For example, in

Lydia answered the door.

the alternative order is possible:

The door Lydia answered (and I answered the telephone).

This is because with a verb like *answer*, which expects a human subject 'doing' the action, a personal name can be identified as the subject. However with a sentence like

Lydia telephoned her parents.

the rearrangement into

Her parents Lydia telephoned.

becomes less possible, since *telephone* expects a person as both subject and object, and in this rearranged version, it is not immediately clear who telephoned whom.

Another way in which sentence elements can be rearranged is by the choice of verb. Compare:

Lydia owns the Mini convertible.
The Mini convertible belongs to Lydia.

'Own' and 'belong to' are counterpart verbs to express ownership: 'own' puts the owner into initial position and the object owned into final, and 'belong to' does the reverse. Other pairs of 'converse' words act similarly; compare:

Rachel sold the Mini convertible to Lydia.
Lydia bought the Mini convertible from Rachel.

and:

The museum is behind the warehouse.
The warehouse is in front of the museum.

In this last case the converses are a pair of prepositions: *behind* and *in front of*.

Fronting

The mechanisms for moving an element to the initial position of a sentence are known as 'fronting'. One way of fronting an element, which we have considered briefly already (Chapter 3), is the 'passive' construction. The basic form of a sentence is 'active': the 'doer' of an 'action' is the subject of the sentence, and the 'victim' is normally the direct object, as in:

Jennifer has insulted Monica.

In the 'passive' form of a sentence, the 'victim' becomes the subject in initial position, and the 'doer' takes up final position in a prepositional phrase introduced with *by*:

Monica has been insulted by Jennifer.

You will also notice that the form of the verb changes. For a sentence to be changed into the passive, the verb must be 'transitive'; that is, it must take an object. A sentence with an intransitive verb, such as *go*, cannot be made passive. For example:

They have gone to the park.

cannot be changed into:

To the park has been gone by them.

or

The park has been gone to by them.

Where a verb can take two objects (direct and indirect), usually either of them can be fronted in a passive version of the sentence. For example:

Jennifer gave Monica an apology.

can become either:

An apology was given (to) Monica by Jennifer (direct object becomes subject).

or:

Monica was given an apology by Jennifer (indirect object becomes subject).

Note again the passive form of the verb: *was given*.

Another mechanism for fronting an element of a sentence and at the same time giving it a measure of emphasis is the so-called 'cleft construction'. The cleft construction splits (cleaves) a sentence in two to provide focus on a fronted element. For example, taking our previous sentence:

It was Monica // to whom Jennifer gave an apology.

Monica is fronted and focused, and the second half of the sentence is introduced by the relative pronoun *whom*, alternatively *that Jennifer gave an apology to*. Any of the noun elements in the sentence could have the same treatment:

It was an apology that Jennifer gave (to) Monica.
It was Jennifer who gave Monica an apology.

Even the subject (*Jennifer*) can have the cleft treatment.

The one item that cannot be clefted by the '*It* + *be* + focus // relative clause' formula is the verb itself. This is remedied by another kind of cleft construction, of the form:

What Jennifer did // was give Monica an apology.

or:

What Jennifer gave (Monica) // was an apology.

The formula here is: '*What* + subject + *do* // *be* ... .'

Postponement

The mechanisms for moving an element to the end of a sentence are known as 'postponement'. The passive construction can be regarded as a mechanism for postponement, as well as for fronting. The item that is postponed is the subject, so *Jennifer* in:

Monica has been insulted by Jennifer.
An apology was given to Monica by Jennifer.

The passive also leaves open the possibility that the 'doer' (or 'agent') can be omitted:

Monica has been insulted.
Monica has been given an apology.

This then locates alternative items in the final position of the sentence: the verb in the first example (*insulted*), and in the second the object that has not been fronted (*an apology*).

The item that fills the initial position in a sentence, besides functioning as the 'theme' or 'topic' of the sentence, is also often an item that has been mentioned in the, or a previous, sentence in the text. It refers to what is called 'given information'. At the most general level, a text can be viewed as a series of sentences with the structure 'given' + 'new' information, where the 'new' information in one sentence becomes the 'given' information in a subsequent sentence. This also implies that 'given' information comes at the beginning of a sentence, making the connection with what has gone before, and 'new' information comes towards the end of a sentence. This is a generalisation, and in reality texts have a much more complex structure and texture than this implies.

What happens when you don't have any 'given' information to start a sentence with, such as at the beginning of a text or a paragraph? You can use an introductory sentence known as an 'existential' sentence, introduced by the word *there*:

There is one further point to consider.
There was a proposal for a new college.
There has been a spate of burglaries in this neighbourhood.

The word *there* stands for the theme, which is postponed, and the sentence serves to state the existence of something, to be elaborated on in subsequent text.

A more obvious and widespread case of postponement is 'extraposition' (literally, 'putting outside'). It operates on sentences that have clauses as subject, for example:

That the liquid in the test tube turned cloudy is surprising.
To classify diseases in this way is useful.

These sentences are unwieldy. In English, the longest element in a sentence tends to go at the end, under the so-called 'principle of end-weight'. Extraposition supports this principle by filling initial position with a 'dummy *it*' and moving the subject clause to the end of the sentence:

It is surprising that the liquid in the test tube turned cloudy.
It is useful to classify diseases in this way.

The clauses that are usually subject to extraposition are *that* clauses and *to* infinitive clauses (see Chapter 4). With *seem* as the main verb in the sentence, extraposition is obligatory:

It seems that the chairman has decided to resign.

but not:

That the chairman has decided to resign seems.

Another way in which a long subject can be made shorter is by postponing part of it. This can happen, for example, if the subject noun phrase contains a relative clause or a comparative phrase or clause:

The family who had disappeared the previous week were found camping in Devon.

could become:

The family were found camping in Devon who had disappeared the previous week.

in which the relative clause *who had disappeared the previous week* is postponed to the end of the sentence. Similarly:

Fewer road accidents have resulted in death or serious injury than last year.

has the postponement of the comparative phrase *than last year* from the subject:

Fewer road accidents than last year have resulted in death or serious injury.

These mechanisms for fronting and postponement demonstrate how sentence elements can be moved around within sentences, especially to fill the important initial and final positions. As you write, the questions to ask are these:

- Does this sentence make connection with those I have already written, so that a reader can easily follow my train of thought?

- Does this sentence announce its topic at or near the beginning, so that a reader immediately grasps what the sentence is about?

- Does this sentence read well? Does it have balance? Are the longer, more weighty elements positioned towards the end?

- If I have ignored the principles of initial 'given' theme or end-focus or end-weight, is the stylistic effect worth it? Or am I likely to confuse my readers?

Reflecting on how you distribute information within a sentence may help you to get your point across more successfully.

An Example

Before you read the commentary that follows, you may like to identify the initial and final elements in each of the numbered sentences and reflect on their function in the developing text.

[1] Stories about the harmful effects of the media are rarely absent from the headlines. [2] In recent weeks, reports have

claimed that watching television retards the development of the brain, produces attention deficit disorder and precipitates early puberty. [3] Meanwhile, the debate about advertising and obesity rumbles on; and the internet is apparently infested with predatory paedophiles busily grooming our children.

[4] For decades, the media have been blamed for causing violent crime, educational underachievement, sexual obsession, political apathy – and just about every other social ill you care to name.

[5] Most of these concerns are overstated, and much of the 'research' on which they are based is barely worthy of the name. [6] Yet as channels proliferate, as global corporations extend their reach, and as technology makes it easier to copy and communicate, there is a growing sense that people's access to the media can no longer be controlled. (opening of an 'opinion' article in the *Guardian* newspaper, 27 July 2004, with sentence numbers inserted)

In sentence 2, the fronted adverbial of time *in recent weeks* connects to *rarely absent* in sentence 1. In sentence 3, the initial *meanwhile* joins this sentence to the previous one by continuing the list of examples of 'harmful effects'. Sentence 4 begins with *for decades*, another adverbial of time, which parallels the *in recent weeks* of sentence 2, extending the time scope of the 'harmful effects'; note, also, the passive construction (*have been blamed*). Sentence 5 has the subject in initial position, with *these concerns* referring back to what has been mentioned in the previous three sentences; again a passive construction is used (*are overstated*). The connection in sentence 6 is made by *yet*, drawing a contrast between what is about to be said and what has gone before. This is an existential *there* sentence, with three adverbials of time introduced by *as* in initial position, before the author introduces a new theme, *a growing sense that* … .

The progression of given and new, theme/topic and comment is not regular and straightforward, but there is a clear progression and a sense that the ordering of the elements within the sentences serves to drive the argument of the text onwards.

Summary

The following terms have been discussed in this chapter. They are all summarised in the Glossary at the end of the book.

theme   rearrangement
fronting   postponement
active/passive   cleft sentence   existential sentence
extraposition
given/new information

6 Sentences into Texts

In the previous chapter we looked at ways in which sentences could be rearranged to make them suitable vehicles for the development of the message of a text. In this chapter we are going to take this approach a step further by looking at how sentences may be incorporated into paragraphs and texts.

Paragraph

The paragraph is a construct of written language. It does not occur in any recognisable form in spoken discourse. Some linguists who have recently studied spoken language in some detail would say the same about the sentence. But it is arguable that sentence-like or clause-like structures are identifiable in spoken language. The sentence remains a useful unit for describing the structural relationships of grammar at this level (subject – verb – object, and so on), and it has some correspondence to how we organise and express our thoughts.

There is no clear 'grammar' of the paragraph as there is of the sentence. There is, in general, no series of possible slots to be filled, as in a sentence; though the initial and final sentences of a paragraph may be significant in the ongoing communication of a text, just as the initial and final slots of a sentence are. In some texts the structure may be more fixed; for example, in recipes there is usually a paragraph for 'ingredients', followed by one for 'method of preparation'. Some forms of academic writing, similarly, have a set pattern: hypothesis, literature review, method, results, interpretation, conclusion. But not all text types are so prescribed.

Paragraphs are, usually, for the choosing. The usual advice is to make a paragraph in some sense self-contained, dealing with a topic or sub-topic in the developing text. However, what exactly counts as a 'topic' is a matter of judgement. Equally, the average size of paragraphs will vary with the type of text: paragraphs in newspapers tend to be much shorter than those in academic textbooks or serious novels; and the size will vary according to the personal style of the author. An influencing factor may be the appearance of the text on the page and the circumstances in which the text is expected to be read: newspapers tend to have narrow columns, so a paragraph soon begins to look rather long, and they are often read fleetingly and selectively in 'noisy' circumstances (on a bus or train). Both of these factors would tend to suggest shorter paragraphs.

In terms of structure, as indicated earlier, it is the initial and final sentences that are significant. As with the initial slot in sentences, the first sentence of a paragraph may make a connection with the previous paragraph in the text, and it will usually set the topic or theme for the paragraph that it is initiating. The final sentence may serve to draw the threads of the paragraph together into a conclusion, and it may also point forward to the next paragraph in the text. In a developing argument the initial sentence may make a proposition, which is then followed by supporting or contradictory evidence, and the final sentence draws a conclusion from the evidence presented. In a developing narrative the initial sentence may introduce an episode in the story, followed by sentences relating the unfolding of the episode, and the final sentence may bring the episode to a conclusion with a denouement, a climax, or a cliffhanger.

Consider these examples, first of a narrative introduction to a feature article from the *Guardian* (28 July 2004):

> One evening in October 1905, a young woman rose to her feet during a Liberal party rally in Manchester's Free Trade Hall. 'Will the Liberal government give votes to women?' she yelled, her foghorn voice belying her slender, almost fragile appearance. When no response came, she clambered on to her seat and repeated the offence, flourishing a home-made banner to ram home the point.

> A few moments later, Annie Kenney and her friend Christabel Pankhurst were outside on the pavement, having been dragged from the hall by outraged party officials. Christabel completed the night's work by spitting in a policeman's face and finally achieving arrest.

While these two paragraphs are part of the same story, the paragraph division is justified on the basis that the story has two episodes: one that takes place inside the hall, and one on the street outside. Notice how both paragraphs begin with an adverbial of time (*One evening in October 1905*, *A few moments later*), placing each episode in a time setting. The first paragraph concludes with the climax of the protest, and in the final sentence of the second note the use of *completed* and *finally* to indicate a conclusion.

The second example is from an argumentative text:

> Two quite separate ideas are colliding in the minds of Spain's anti-religious socialists. Modern Spain, a secular state, has been struggling for the last three decades to achieve the separation of church and state, and make the Catholic church in Spain self-financing. As part of a deal in 1979 that was supposed to be temporary, taxpayers were given the right to decide whether they wanted a share of their taxes – 0.5239% – to be given to the church, with the state making up the rest of the church's needs. Today the tax meets only one third of the church's budget, and more and more questions are being asked about the need to subsidise Catholic worshippers, when growing numbers of Spanish Protestants, Muslims, and Jews receive no subsidy. Spain is, after all, a country that will legalise gay marriage, relax rules on abortion, and encourage stem cell research with human embryos.

> The second idea arises from the March 11 bombings and bloody siege of a flat in which the leader of the al-Qaida cell, Sarhane Ben Abdelmajid Fakhet, blew up himself, fellow bombers and a police officer. A shredded videotape recovered from the scene revealed that Fakhet's cell called itself 'the brigade situated in al Andalus' – the Arabic name for the part of the Iberian peninsula that remained in Muslim hands until the Reconquista in 1492. However mad the thought might be that the bombings were a reprise of a religious war that ended 500 years ago, it is making the government rethink the state's relationship with its Muslim population and with Morocco. Spain is once again seeing itself as the bridge between the Islamic world and the west. Whether funding mosques will lead to better relations with Muslim immigrants remains to be seen. Being a secular state, the other route Spain could take is to cut off all links with all churches.

These are the second and third paragraphs from a leader article in the *Guardian*, 28 July 2004. The first sentence of the first of these paragraphs introduces 'two ... ideas'. The first idea is elaborated in the first of the paragraphs, and the second idea in the subsequent paragraph. The first sentence of the second paragraph introduces this second idea. The final sentence of the first paragraph serves to round off the first point about Spain's secular state. The final sentence of the second paragraph reiterates this and brings the discussion to a conclusion with a suggestion to resolve the issue that has been raised and expanded on.

Sentence Connections

We saw in the previous chapter how the links between clauses within sentences could be made explicit by means of co-ordinating (*and, but*) and subordinating (*if, because, while*) conjunctions. A similar, indeed more extensive, set of items exists for making explicit connections between sentences, within a paragraph or even across paragraphs. These items are words such as *moreover* and *however* (called 'conjunctive adverbs'). The connections that they make fall into four broad types of relation: 'additive' (an *and* relation), 'adversative' (a *but* relation), 'causal' (a *so* relation), and 'temporal' (a *then* relation).

A sentence introduced by an additive connector, such as *furthermore, additionally, moreover, besides*, may simply be adding further information to the preceding text:

1 Funding the Beveridge plan was supposed to be no problem. *Moreover*, Keynes seemed to be saying that high levels of public spending were a guarantee of peace-time full employment. (FLOB Corpus, J58)

2 You should be in no danger. *Besides*, someone in your profession must surely expect to run some risks. (FLOB N18)

Additive connection is also taken to include: specifying alternatives:

3 The motive power for the hydraulic motors for a number of gates could be provided by a single power source. *Alternatively*, each gate could have its own power source. (FLOB J73)

providing asides:

4   Use the word 'you' — it makes direct contact with your audience. *Incidentally*, try and avoid too much reference to yourself and limit the use of the word 'I'. (FLOB F03)

rephrasing:

5   It is also generally accepted that these ascriptions of mental states are theoretical. *In other words*, it is always possible for them to be wrong. (FLOB G63)

exemplification:

6   The cultural context could have been usefully elaborated further. *For instance*, it is important to understand the length of term for which a mayor is elected, and in particular the role of the mayor's political office and its director. (FLOB E32)

and comparison:

7   Whereas some small shops are excellent and very friendly, others are tatty and uninviting. *Similarly*, some supermarkets are unkempt with poor stock control and long check-out queues, but others are clean, well-stocked, and brimming with good service … . (FLOB B25)

Although frowned on by some people, *and* itself can also function as an additive connection at the beginning of a sentence:

8   It was the first time she had witnessed such raw and naked grief; it was also her first experience of the death of someone close. *And* there was the awesome realization that her husband had very nearly been killed too. (FLOB G31)

All these examples connect sentences within a paragraph. Here is an example of *moreover* connecting paragraphs within a text:

9   Yet the equity orientation of UK pension funds has relied heavily on the willingness of British companies to adopt a high pay-out strategy. That has led to criticism from the UK corporate sector on the grounds that continental and Japanese companies do not face the same pressures from their own institutional shareholders.

> *Moreover* the entry of the UK to full membership of the European Monetary System six months ago posed the possibility of fundamental structural change. (FLOB A15)

All the examples also illustrate the use of the connecting adverb in first position in the sentence. In this position the connection is made most explicitly and immediately. The adverb may, however, occur within the sentence, though usually near the beginning, and surrounded by commas:

10 One of the general weaknesses of Bultmann's theology is that its austere challenge is issued directly to each individual, poor, bare, forked, human animal in isolation from all the rest. It has, *in other words*, virtually no social dimension. What is more, it is curiously timeless. (FLOB D01)

The third sentence is included here to illustrate a further additive connection, *what is more*.

General adversative connection is achieved with adverbs like *yet, however, nevertheless, though*:

1 The EC also recently extended its customs union to include EFTA states into a European Economic Area. *However* everyone understands that for all the EFTA states this is only a way-station toward full Community membership. (FLOB F11)

2 He argued further that this system could not be learnt from the environment by any conventional learning procedure. *Nevertheless* it must be possible for children to acquire these rules because children evidently do learn a language. (FLOB J23)

3 Unfortunately I lost touch with her when I was seventeen so I can't help. What stunned me, *though*, was how he'd found me after all this time. (FLOB L04)

Other adversatives include: *on the other hand*:

4 Exploitation of the world's land has been described by some as conforming to a 'lollipop model', in that, with each 'lick', there is less for the future. *On the other hand*, with good management, it might

be possible to sustain indefinite usage of land, even improve its utility. (FLOB J03)

on the contrary:

5 'There is nothing to discuss,' she said, a little wearily ... 'There is, **on the contrary**, a great deal to be discussed, my dear child ... .' (FLOB P01)

instead:

6 He rejected hereditary monarchy, aristocracy or the mixed form of government Britain enjoyed in the eighteenth century. *Instead*, he favoured a representative democracy and a republican form of government. (FLOB F30)

Similarly, *but* can function as an adversative link between sentences, though, as with *and*, it is frowned on by some people:

7 In Gibson's *Hamlet*, as in nearly every version since the Stoppard play, the expression of royal gratitude to the pair — King Claudius: 'Thanks, Rosencrantz and gentle Guildenstern'; Queen Gertrude: 'Thanks, Guildenstern and gentle Rosencrantz' — has the emphasis of the consort correcting the monarch, although there is no stage direction to that effect. Gertrude could well have reversed the names out of pure politeness.

   But confusion of identity is the precise target of Stoppard's humour. (FLOB C08)

This also illustrates the use of a conjunction to join two paragraphs within a text. The use of *but* in positions like this draws a powerful contrast.

The causal relationship adduces reasons or expresses consequences that follow from a previous sentence or portion of text. The typical conjunctions are *(and) so, therefore, consequently*:

1 He returned from studying in France in the early '60s with a fiery desire to produce wines fit to compete with the best in the world.

And so he imported foreign grapes, initially the Bordeaux classics, and started producing a number of thoroughly atypical, un-Spanish wines. (FLOB E20)

2 However, one positive thing at least emerges from all the attacks the corporation has to endure — namely the significant position it has in our culture. It goes without saying, *therefore*, that the image the BBC projects is extremely important. (FLOB E35)

Note that *therefore* is not initial in the sentence, a position it takes up less frequently than internally. This example is also interesting because both sentences contain a connecting adverb.

3 DB designed the railway for operation at 300 km/h with an ultimate goal in mind of 350 km/h. *Consequently*, large diameter tunnels were planned (cross-section 82 m²) to limit the pressure problem and to ease traction energy costs associated with aerodynamic drag. (FLOB J74)

A conclusion may also be drawn with *hence*:

4 They cannot tolerate mistakes or the lack of proper initiatives from the workers. *Hence* in this context they will specify contracts that require a high level of effort. (FLOB J45)

A consequence, or 'result', may be expressed by *as a result*, usually in formal writing:

5 Placental insufficiency can also happen if the mother's circulatory system is not working properly because of high blood pressure or other chronic disease. *As a result*, the baby does not get enough oxygen or nourishment, becomes weak and does not grow properly. (FLOB F31)

Similarly, a purpose may be introduced by *to this end*:

6 'We are looking for wines with a winey character,' says Michael Trull, 'wines that are good with food and not excessively floral; more French than German.' *To this end*, Trull believes in the importance

of blending to produce a consistent style, neither overly Germanic, nor slavishly following the New World cult of the grape variety. (FLOB E05)

Temporal connection, like adverbial clauses of time within sentences, links events in time. The connection may be sequential, with *(and) then* or *next*:

1 Paul had said that a woman was on her way, travelling with two children, but my flight was booked before she was due.

   Then suddenly I saw this smiling, open face, fair hair flying, blue jeans, pink shirt. (FLOB D06)

In this case, the connection takes place across a paragraph boundary. The relation may be one of previous time:

2 The job record is transmitted to the Accounts Department for job costing so that delays between completion of work and invoicing are kept to a minimum. *Previously*, collating, totalling and checking this information manually took ten man hours a day. (FLOB J80)

or of simultaneous time:

3 The EPLF had moved to within 30 miles of Assab, keeping the government troops there fully occupied.

   At the same time, rebels of the Ethiopian Peoples' Revolutionary Democratic Front, made up of liberation movements from the Tigray, Afar and Oromo ethnic groups, intensified their push towards Addis Ababa. (FLOB A20)

The connection is again made across a paragraph boundary.

There are numerous ways of making an explicit time link between sentences, in addition to those mentioned; for example *after that, thereupon, after a time, next day, meanwhile, from now on*, and so on. Another use of some of these, and other, connectors is to make logical, rather than strictly time, connections and to map a path through an argument text. This can be done with connectors like *then* and *next*, or more explicitly still with enumerators like *first(ly), second(ly), finally*:

4   This book looks in detail at the development of the Christian church in China since the Cultural Revolution (1966–76). *First* we examine the Cultural Revolution period itself, which witnessed both extreme persecution and the embryonic growth of vigorous spiritual life (chs 2–3). *Secondly* the new religious policy of the Chinese Communist Party is analysed in depth from the original sources, both at the national and local levels (chs 4-5). (FLOB F25)

5   When your article is finished, reading it aloud helps you notice the uncomfortable phrases, the pomposities, the waffle and the repetitions. Delete them all. Tighten up your writing; it can only be better.

Finally, type your article and the associated captions sheet, double-spaced (type a line, miss a line) on white A4 paper, leaving wide margins. (FLOB E10)

After a series of instructions on how to prepare an article for a magazine, the author reaches a last set and introduces the paragraph with *finally*.

In example 4, the final phrase should more correctly read: *both at the national and at the local level* or *at both the national and the local level*. Constructions with 'correlative conjunctions', such as *both … and* or *either … or*, require repeated or parallel items.

We have gone into some detail on this topic and given a large number of examples of different kinds of conjunction because this is an important way in which you can guide a reader through your text and ensure that they make the connections that you want them to make and understand your text in the way that you intended it. It is worthwhile cultivating the judicious use of conjunctive adverbs; they are especially valuable in texts that are proposing an argument or attempting to persuade a reader of an opinion or a point of view, such as most academic essays.

Paragraph and Text

We have said that paragraphs are for the choosing, but we have seen that there are some principles to structuring paragraphs in different types of text, as well as means of making explicit connections between sentences and between paragraphs. We might next ask if there are any principles of organisation that govern the structure of texts in terms of the paragraphs that compose them.

Different principles apply according to the type of text. In broad terms, a descriptive text (of a house in an estate agent's particulars) differs from a narrative text (a novel) differs from an expository text (academic text-book) differs from an argumentative text (opinions column in a news-paper) differs from an instructive text (a DIY manual). A narrative text, for example, would be expected to have chronology as its overriding organisational principle. Most narratives would also be expected to lead towards a climax and possibly a denouement. An argumentative text, on the other hand, would have logical deduction as its overriding principle of organisation, with the presentation of theses, evidence and conclusion. A text may contain features of two or more of these broad types.

Let us look at an example:

> A few weeks ago I wrote about a Japanese couple who visited their native Japan for the first time and were amazed to find the extent to which lotus is grown as a commercial crop. They confessed to surprise at finding entire hillsides a patch-work of lotus fields. But I did not have enough space to men-tion that other typical Japanese crop – seaweed.
>
> She writes: 'In many of the bays around the Pacific coast there is an extensive yet delicate tracery of bamboo or brush-wood screens sticking up out of the sea. The seaweed which is cultivated on them is pre-cut into small rectangles and packed airtight. The brittle, dark shiny green weed forms a nutritious wrapping for rice balls, many of which are eaten at breakfast along with fish.'
>
> Now it seems that seaweed is enjoying a vogue in Britain. At the moment there are four varieties fairly readily available in supermarkets. They are dulse, nori, *haricots de la mer* and green sea-lettuce or green laver. Nori and *haricots de la mer* are tasteless if eaten raw. In supermarkets they come in deep, plastic cartons, damp and glistening with crystals of rock salt. The other two are supplied in delicate sheets, and green sea-lettuce may even be eaten raw. Fortunately, unlike wild fungi, they are quite harmless. Palatability is the only criterion.

Fresh seaweed, though known to the crofters of Scotland and Ireland, is a novelty to the English public but may see an upsurge of popularity. Chefs are experimenting with sauces and seasoning, and a winner seems to be any firm-fleshed white fish or prawns, served hot with only pepper and salt and seaweed as garnishing. But it has a long way to go before it is generally accepted. (Ralph Whitlock, *Guardian Weekly*, 6 August 1995)

This is the opening of the text. It is framed by a narrative structure: *a few weeks ago*; but it then moves into description of the various kinds of edible seaweed available in supermarkets. A sort of narrative thread is kept alive by *now*, introducing the third paragraph, and by the verb phrase *are experimenting* in the final paragraph. So, this text has features of both the narrative (moving through time) and the descriptive (static state of affairs) types. Notice, too, how the information is distributed among the paragraphs:

1 introduction to bring up the topic of seaweed

2 what the correspondent writes

3 description of available seaweeds

4 prognostication of whether seaweed will catch on in England.

Each one can be regarded as a self-contained topic, yet all form part of an overall theme.

EXERCISE

Reconstructing text

The following paragraphs from a newspaper text have been jumbled up. Put them in the correct order; and reflect on the cues that enabled you to reconstruct the text.

[1] 'That anyone under 16 should be in the West End of London unaccompanied after 9pm does not seem a good idea,' he said. 'I don't think any responsible parent would like their 15-year-old wandering about at night.'

[2] Glen Smyth, chairman of the Metropolitan Police Federation, said it was better to have the powers than not. But he admitted there could be problems enforcing them. 'Some of these kids may not have parents at home or their parents may not care where they are at night.'

[3] Police are to use new powers to pick up under-16s in the West End of London after 9pm and take them home to their parents, it was revealed yesterday.

[4] Sir Ian Blair, the Metropolitan Police deputy commissioner, denied the police were spoiling teenagers' fun. He said the pilot schemes, a number of which have been agreed between police forces and local authorities throughout England and Wales under anti-social behaviour legislation, were aimed at safeguarding youngsters and stopping gangs causing trouble.

[5] Christine Atkinson, police adviser to the NSPCC, said: 'We don't want to see the West End turned into a no-go area for young people. However, we would support any initiative which helps vulnerable young people in London.'

[6] 'We've now reached a position where the largest capital in Europe is out of bounds at night to thousands of young people,' he said. 'Don't have the lunacy of London under curfew while Baghdad is not.'

[7] Supporters of the plan said it would help police tackle unruly gangs and protect vulnerable children. But critics condemned it as a waste of officers' time and an infringement of civil rights.

[8] Scotland Yard has designated 16 'dispersal areas' across the capital where officers can impose a curfew on unaccompanied minors.

[9] But Barry Hugill, director of the civil rights group Liberty, said it was 'lunacy' and called for a legal challenge.

[10] Another police source, who did not want to be named, said: 'We don't want to be turned into a glorified taxi service. What if this takes us away from a real problem?'

[11] He said Liberty estimated that 70% of the UK was now under curfew. 'There is no denying there are problems with rowdy youngsters but this penalises the majority of well-behaved teenagers because of the wrongdoing minority.'

[12] These include tourist spots such as Oxford Street, Regent Street, Trafalgar Square and Piccadilly Circus, and the neighbour-hoods around Paddington and Victoria.

[13] Sir Ian said residents welcomed the plan. One elderly man in Camden said he had been able to sleep properly for the first time in 10 years.

[14] Thousands of teenagers flock to the West End's cinemas, cafés and burger bars every evening and many films and theatre performances do not even start until after 9pm.

The paragraphs in this text, because it is a news article from a newspaper (The *Guardian*, 30 July 2004), are generally very short. There may be more than one way in which they can be rearranged. The solution can be found below.

Summary

The following terms have been introduced in this chapter. You can check them in the Glossary.

text	paragraph
conjunctive adverb	
additive connection	adversative connection
causal connection	temporal (time) connection

SOLUTIONS TO EXERCISES

Reconstructing text

The order of the paragraphs in the original text was:

$$3 - 8 - 12 - 7 - 14 - 4 - 1 - 13 - 9 - 6 - 11 - 2 - 10 - 5.$$

Some of the cues that may have helped you:

- [3] is a typical opener to a newspaper report, giving a general summary of the story that is to follow.
- [8] begins with 'Scotland Yard', a regular synonym of 'Police' at the beginning of [3].
- [12] begins with the pronoun 'These', which invites the reader to connect to a preceding plural noun or nouns; and the sentence contains a number of place names that link to 'areas' in [8].
- [7] must come soon after [3] and [8], because these must be what 'the plan' refers to.
- [14], while linking to the topic, begins a new section of the text.
- [4] contains the 'teenagers' link to [14].
- [1] continues quoting the deputy commissioner from [4].
- [13] continues the quote, repeating 'Sir Ian's' name at the beginning.
- [9] begins with an adversative 'But', to present a contrast with what has just been said (by the police deputy commissioner).
- [6] continues Mr Hugill's (the 'he' of this sentence) opinions, and the repetition of 'lunacy' links the two paragraphs.
- [11] continues what 'he' (Mr Hugill) said, and the reference to 'Liberty' makes the connection.
- [2] gives an alternative opinion, but conceding some problems with enforcing the law; so it naturally comes later than Sir Ian Blair's positive endorsement.
- [10] cites 'another' police source, implying that at least one has preceded it.
- [5] quotes another authority. These opinions, presumably provided for 'balance', could have perhaps come in a different order.

Getting Your Point Across

In this chapter we are going to pick up on some of the points mentioned in earlier chapters, as well as a few others, and provide some advice on how to make grammar work for you, so that your essays and reports communicate effectively what you want to say.

There are two general principles that underlie effective writing:

1   **accuracy in grammatical expression, punctuation and spelling, so that your reader is not distracted by any such mistakes**

2   **a style that is straightforward and easy to follow, and which does not overburden the reader with needing to guess at what you mean.**

Writing is not like speech. When you are talking to another person in the give and take of dialogue, you always have the possibility of seeking clarification, and you often know the person you are talking to and so can guess at what they are wanting to say. In writing, you can usually make no assumptions about who might be reading your composition, and they cannot ask you for immediate clarification if something is obscure or ambiguous. As a writer, you need to do everything you can to make sure that your reader will be able to understand your message without the possibility of confusion or misinterpretation. In other words, you need to adhere to the normal conventions of spelling, grammar and punctuation in order not to obscure your message.

We will look at spelling and punctuation in Chapter 9. Here, we will make some suggestions about grammar and about style.

Grammar: Ten Things To Avoid

INCOMPLETE SENTENCES

We noted in Chapter 4 that sentences contain a minimum of a subject and a verb, and maybe more, depending on the choice of verb. We also noted that a subordinate clause cannot stand on its own as a sentence: it needs to be attached to a main clause in some way. To be avoided, therefore, are sentences with no verb:

> Against all expectations the mixture in the test tube exploded. An absolute catastrophe.

This could be rewritten as:

> Against all expectations the mixture in the test tube exploded, which was an absolute catastrophe.

or as:

> Against all expectations the mixture in the test tube exploded. This was an absolute catastrophe.

Similarly, a lone subordinate clause should be avoided:

> For – and here I come at last to the very heart of my subject – the Czechs and Poles have always shared the culture of Western Europe, including its music. Whereas the Russians began to do so only in the second half of the eighteenth century.

The second sentence begins with the subordinating conjunction *whereas*, which seems to be the one most vulnerable to this treatment. The author of this text (LOB J68) actually wrote, correctly:

> For – and here I come at last to the very heart of my subject – the Czechs and Poles have always shared the culture of Western Europe, including its music, whereas the Russians began to do so only in the second half of the eighteenth century.

Here is a further example, this time genuine, from an optician's leaflet:

> Whatever your lifestyle and prescription requirements we can advise on the best and most suitable lenses. Whether you wear them for driving, watching television, reading or even playing sport.

The clause introduced by *whether* should, of course, be attached to the main clause that precedes it, just separated by a comma.

If you have a subordinate clause, make sure that it is attached to its main clause. You may have heard it said that you should not begin a sentence with words like 'because' or 'whether' (that is, a subordinating conjunction). However, provided the subordinate clause that you are beginning a sentence with is followed by a main clause, this proscription does not apply:

> Whereas everything in Boccaccio is hard, elegant and general, // in Chaucer it is muted, peculiar, full of objects that are unexpected and yet oddly characteristic. (LOB C06)

The boundary between the subordinate *whereas* clause and the main clause is marked by //.

RUN-ON SENTENCES

This is almost the opposite problem to the incomplete sentence. It is where a sentence is composed of a series of clauses, separated only by commas:

> Then he told her how he had been bewitched by a wicked witch, how no one could have delivered him from the well but herself, that tomorrow they would go together into his kingdom, then they went to sleep, next morning when the sun awoke them, a carriage came driving up with eight white horses, which had white ostrich feathers on their heads, were harnessed with golden chains, behind them stood the young king's servant Faithful Henry.

This has been adapted, to make the point, from a Grimms' fairy tale. You will notice how difficult it is to work out easily exactly what is going on. The original was clearer, but even here, as in much story telling, there is a tendency to run on:

> Then he told her how he had been bewitched by a wicked witch, and how no one could have delivered him from the well but herself, and that tomorrow they would go together into his kingdom. Then they went to sleep, and next morning when the sun awoke them, a carriage came driving up with eight white horses, which had white ostrich feathers on their heads, and were harnessed with golden chains, and behind stood the young king's servant Faithful Henry.

Apart from a sentence break, the connections between the clauses are made more explicit by the co-ordinating conjunction *and*, but it makes for a rather simplistic style of story telling. The moral, therefore, is not to write long sentences in which the clauses are linked merely by commas. In academic writing, especially, texts need to be more carefully crafted, and connections between clauses need to be made explicit. You cannot expect your reader to do all the interpretation. In general, overlong sentences should be avoided.

LONG SUBJECTS

While we are on the subject of length, here is another long element to avoid: long subjects. We noted in Chapter 5 that subjects composed of finite clauses (*that* clauses and *wh-* clauses) tend to be extraposed, and that relative clauses in subject noun phrases may be postponed. Long subjects normally consist of heavily modified noun phrases or of clauses:

> An open letter written by Earl Russell hoping that the President's visit to London 'will prove fruitful' was handed in at the American Embassy by representatives of the Committee of 100. (LOB A04)

The subject extends from *An* to *fruitful*. The head noun is *letter*, and it is followed by two non-finite clauses: *written by Earl Russell* and *hoping that …fruitful*. Arguably this produces an overlong subject, keeping the reader waiting too long for the main verb, *was handed in*. It could be rewritten as:

An open letter had been written by Earl Russell, which hoped that the President's visit to London 'will prove fruitful'. It was handed in at the American Embassy by representatives of the Committee of 100.

or as:

An open letter, which had been written by Earl Russell, was handed in at the American Embassy by representatives of the Committee of 100. It hoped that the President's visit to London 'will prove fruitful'.

Now here is an example of a clausal subject:

That the growth of the other stars has been largely a result of wise American statesmanship in the past does not make the present situation any easier. (LOB B18)

The subject clause extends from *That* to *past*, making a very front-heavy sentence. The reader waits a long time for the main verb, *does not make*. The obvious way to solve the problem is to extrapose the subject clause:

It does not make the present situation any easier that the growth of the other stars has been largely a result of wise American statesmanship in the past.

If the reader has to wait too long for the main verb, especially if the subject contains a clause, either on its own or as part of the post-modification of a noun phrase, then there is a danger that the reader will lose the thread of what you are saying.

DANGLING CLAUSES AND PHRASES

If you begin a sentence with a non-finite clause or a phrase, it must make sense in relation to the subject that follows. Look at these two examples from the optician's leaflet cited above:

Made from the latest materials such as Titanium and using advanced technology, you can choose frames that are strong, feather light and comfortable.

Full of style and very fashionable, we know that we will have a style to suit your image and the shape of your face.

In the first of these examples, the subject is *you*, and the expectation would be that the preceding non-finite clauses, *made from* ... and *using* ..., would relate to *you*. Presumably, though, *made from* ... relates to the object *frames*; and it is not clear what *using* ... could relate to, since there is no noun referring to a 'user'. In the second example, the subject is *we*, and you would expect that the initial phrase, *full of style and very fashionable*, would relate to *we*. It is not entirely clear which element the phrase does relate to: the only candidate would seem to be *style*, but it doesn't quite make sense.

Such clauses and phrases at the beginning of a sentence are said to be 'dangling', since they are not attached to the element that immediately follows them, usually the subject of the sentence. Such constructions are to be avoided if you want your writing to make sense.

COMPLEXITY

Your thought patterns may not always be as well developed, highly organised and logical as you would like them to be, and the confusion in your mind is in danger of being reflected in complex and tortuous sentence structures. The answer, of course, is to sort out the thoughts first, perhaps by setting them down on paper and then ordering them, before committing yourself to writing them in your essay or report. Here is an example of what I consider to be over-complex sentence structure:

This is a continuing problem, for if new frequency bands should be brought into use for additional or colour programmes another crop of aerials can be expected, and although at the much higher frequencies likely to be concerned the rods of the aerials will be only about one foot long, outdoor aerials erected clear of buildings are likely to be necessary even quite near to powerful transmitters.

It is therefore important for the appearance of estates that local authorities and other large property owners should bear in mind that, in conjunction with the local Post Office engineers, it is often possible to do a great deal to mitigate the nuisance; and they should take every opportunity to do so.

The first of these sentences is the one in focus, but the second is included to show that the writer of this text (LOB H22) has a generally convoluted style. Let us attempt to diagram the first sentence:

This is a continuing problem
  for
    if new frequency bands should be brought into use for additional or colour programmes
    another crop of aerials can be expected
    and
    although at the much higher frequencies likely to be concerned the rods of the aerials will be only about one foot long
    outdoor aerials erected clear of buildings are likely to be necessary
    even quite near to powerful transmitters.

I would suggest that the writer would have been well advised to have made two or three separate sentences out of this single long one.

THE WRONG KIND OF RELATIVE

We have talked about relative clauses before, in Chapters 2 and 4. This is to reiterate the point that, when you use a relative clause, you need to be careful that you use the correct relative pronoun and the appropriate punctuation for whether the relative clause is defining or non-defining. Consider the following two examples, both as in their original texts. Which is 'defining' and which 'non-defining'? You will note that neither has the relative clause (introduced by *whom*) separated by commas.

> We shall still remember that they gave their lives to ensure that some of the Europeans whom we are now joining by negotiation, did not conquer us by force. (FLOB B26)
>
> Jan Josef Liefers' self-loving Orsino looks curiously like Cesario whom he clasps to his bosom and cradles lovingly in his lap. (FLOB A18)

In the first example the relative clause, *whom we are now joining by negotiation*, could be defining which 'Europeans' are being talked about. In that case, it should have no comma, either before *whom* (which it doesn't), or at the end (which it does). It is possible to interpret the relative clause as non-defining, if *the Europeans* is being used in the sense of the European Community. It would then need a comma both before and after. What the writer has not done is to make clear to us readers how the relative clause is to be interpreted. Indeed, they have confused us by inserting a comma at the end of the clause.

In the second example, the relative clause is unambiguously non-defining. There is only one 'Cesario' (in Shakespeare's *Twelfth Night*), and so the relative clause should have been preceded by a comma. However, since there could be no ambiguity here, the writer has not so much given us a problem of interpretation as merely broken a convention. To abide by the convention, as we have become aware, and so to be unambiguous in all circumstances, requires an understanding of the rather complex grammar of relative clauses. It is worth making the effort to understand it, in the interests of writing with the utmost clarity.

TOO MUCH NOMINALISATION

This is about whether to use a noun or a verb, and especially about nouns that have been formed out of verbs. For example, do you say 'the proposal for the prevention of' or 'they propose to prevent'? Look at the following examples:

> ... *reintroduction* of *conscription* is far less likely than the *resort* to nuclear weapons ...

> It was shown to be effective in the *treatment* and *prevention* of acute GVHD ...

> ... including such official acts as the *imprisonment* or *deportation* of Iraqi nationals ...

> ... to co-ordinate effective *arrangements* for the *reception* and *resettlement* of refugees

They will publish targets for how long their residents will have to wait for *admission* for *treatment*.

All these examples are from texts in FLOB. The nominalisations are in italics. Let us attempt to rewrite them using verbs instead of nouns:

It is far less likely that they will *reintroduce* conscription than *resort* to nuclear weapons.

It was shown to be effective for *treating* and *preventing* acute GVHD.

... including such official acts as *imprisoning* or *deporting* Iraqi nationals ...

... *to arrange* in an effective and co-ordinated way for *receiving* and *resettling* refugees

They will publish targets for how long their residents will have to wait *to be admitted to be treated*.

The equivalent verbs are in italics. It is not always appropriate to turn a noun into a verb. In the first example, it is difficult to do so for *conscription*, and in the last example it may have been better to have left *treatment*.

Why is too much nominalisation to be avoided? First, a verb usually comes over as more direct and lively; nominalised verbs give an impression of stasis. Second, more than one nominalisation together begins to make a sentence rather dense and difficult to assimilate. A nominalised style is typical of academic writing, but it is less engaging for the reader than when nominalisations are used sparingly.

THE WRONG PREPOSITION

Many verbs, adjectives and nouns in English are followed by a particular preposition. There is usually very little choice about which preposition to use, but it is often the case that writers are confused about which preposition can be used. Here are a few examples from the large set of prepositional verbs:

ask after, ask for, consist of, gamble on, interfere with, look into, object to, quarrel with, speculate about, unload onto, vanish from, wriggle out of.

There are fewer adjectives and nouns that are followed by prepositions; here are some examples:

adept at, afraid of, different from/to, lenient towards, salient to, upset about, worthy of

decision about/on, division into, freedom from, necessity for, treatment for, vestige of.

If you are unsure which preposition is appropriate after a verb, adjective or noun that you are using, you should look the word up in a good dictionary (see Chapter 10).

ARCHAISMS AND OTHER STRANGE WORDS

This is about word choice rather than grammar strictly speaking. Make sure that the words you use are appropriate to the text that you are writing. You will, of course, have to use the technical terms of your subject: being educated in a discipline involves learning its jargon. But, unless you are a lawyer, avoid using archaic-sounding words like *aforementioned* or *heretofore*. And even if you are a lawyer, make sure that they are used only in appropriate contexts, in legal texts not in the exposition of your essay.

Neither should you import into your academic essays words that are slang or very colloquial (*gonna, hip*), nor the abbreviations that you may use in emailing or text messaging (*c u l8er*). Academic prose is less stuffy and formal than it used to be, but it is still at the formal end of the continuum of styles, and features of more informal styles should be avoided.

While we are considering the influence of speech, note that the item which follows modal auxiliaries like *must* and *would* is *have*, not *of*; so it's *must have* and *would have* (not *must of* and *would of*).

You should also avoid making up words. One that I have found a number of students using recently is *proceeding* to mean the opposite of *preceding*.

Proceed means 'to continue with an action' or 'to go in some particular direction'; it does not have the meaning of 'to follow'. Consequently, the present participle *proceeding* cannot be used as an adjective meaning 'following', even though it might look as if it forms a neat counterpart to *preceding*. The common misspelling of *precede* as 'preceed' compounds the confusion.

LEAVING YOUR READER GUESSING

This point picks up on the discussion in Chapters 5 and 6 about making connections between sentences and between paragraphs in a text. A number of resources were outlined there, including those for rearranging the elements in a sentence to aid the flow of information, and those for making explicit the connections between sentences, in the form of conjunctions and conjunctive adverbs. The more dense and 'academic' a text is, the more closely argued an essay is, the greater is the need for guiding your reader by providing continuity and connection in the developing text. In other words, don't leave your reader guessing.

Language Change

The preceding points contain advice that applies to academic writing. Any language, English included, has a diverse range of varieties and styles. What may be regarded as appropriate in one variety (regional dialect, colloquial) may not be acceptable in another (academic essay). Moreover, all languages change over time, not only by increasing the vocabulary to cope with innovations in technology, society and culture, but also in usage that is deemed acceptable in different varieties. Let me take two examples.

The first relates to the difference, mentioned in Chapter 1, between *less* and *fewer*. Two or three decades ago, most people would have said:

There are fewer documentary programmes on television these days.

but:

There is less serious political discussion on television.

Fewer was used with 'countable' nouns like *programme*, while *less* was used with 'uncountable' nouns like *discussion*. Note that in this example *discussion* is being used in its 'mass', abstract sense, rather than in its more concrete sense, which is countable (*fewer serious discussions*), referring to instances of discussion. These days most people use *less* for both countable and uncountable cases:

There are less documentary programmes on television these days.

This loss of distinction between *less* and *fewer* is more recently being transferred to the similar pair of words *number* and *amount*. Conventionally, we would say:

There is (are?) a large number of people in the room.

but:

There is a large amount of mail on the doormat.

The same distinction applies between 'countable' (*number*) and 'uncountable' (*amount*). The current tendency is to use *amount* for both, so:

There is a large amount of people in the room.

For some like me, who have a fairly conservative usage, this is, as yet, a change too far. In students' essays I no longer correct *less* where *fewer* was usual, but I do still correct *amount* where *number* is required. No doubt, I shall get used to this change in time.

What this points up, however, is that you need to be aware that the person reading or marking your essay may have more conservative linguistic usage than you have, and that this may have an effect on how they read your composition.

My second example is of a different kind, and it relates to the formality/ informality distinction. Consider these two sentences from a leader article in the broadsheet *Guardian* newspaper (for 6 August 2004):

At long last there are also tentative signs of a revival of something you don't hear a lot about these days – the house building market.

Wherever you look, however, it is difficult to see a case for interest rates to continue rising much further.

Notice that the first sentence contains the contracted form *don't* (instead of *do not*), but the second sentence contains the full form *it is* (rather than the contracted form *it's*). Leaders are where you tend to find the most formal language in a newspaper, and it is interesting to find this inconsistency in such a text. It is symptomatic of the uncertainty today about the extent to which contractions like *don't* and *it's* (the two most common) should be allowed in formal texts. I have noticed such contractions in international academic journals, but in general they are still frowned on in formal academic writing. This is a changing usage: fifty years ago, contractions would have occurred very infrequently in newspapers, and then mainly in direct quotations; today, they can be found in all types of newspapers and in all types of newspaper texts. They are far less tolerated in academic writing; you will need to make a judgment about whether those who will be reading your work would frown on contractions.

What emerges from this discussion is the following:

- Each variety of English (speech/writing, dialect/standard, colloquial/ formal) has its own norms of usage — you need to be aware of those for academic writing.

- Language changes and norms of usage change.

- An older generation (your tutors) is likely to have more 'conservative' norms of usage than the younger (you).

- You need to be conscious that something you regard as all right in formal writing may not be viewed as such by your tutors.

EXERCISE

Here is a piece of 'poor' writing, containing a number of the errors discussed in the chapter. Rewrite it, correcting what you perceive as poor grammar; and then compare yours with the version that follows.

Active Community is the Union's Volunteer Programme which aims to create a positive experience for students and local people through volunteering and developing a truly 'active community'. It offers you the chance for personal growth. Giving you valuable skills and experience. As well as a chance to make a real difference in people's lives.

We have dedicated staff across all the campuses to guide you through the process and help you make the right choice for you so it doesn't matter where you're based, you will be given a basic induction so you know what is expected of you and what support you can expect from us. Your expenses will be covered so volunteering won't cost you anything. Volunteering is a two way process where volunteers gain as much from their experiences as the people they work with.

It is crucial to find a Volunteering Opportunity, which matches your skills and interests, and therefore we have a continually expanding, wide range of opportunities available with various charities and organisations. Don't worry, we will help you pick the right placement for you, to fit in with your needs and you're schedule, so you get the most out of it! If we don't currently offer something that you really want we will do our best to find something for you.

(Adapted from a text appearing on a students union website.)

Rewriting:

Active Community is the Union's Volunteer Programme, which aims to create a positive experience for students and local people through your volunteering and our developing a truly 'active community'. [Insert comma before 'which', because it is a non-defining relative clause; insert 'your' before 'volunteering' to make clear that it is the students and not the local people who will be volunteers, and 'our' before 'developing' to show this is a co-operative venture.] It offers you the chance for personal growth, giving you valuable skills and experience, as well as a chance to make a real difference in people's lives. [Incorporate the stranded subordinate clauses ('giving ...' and 'as well as ...') into the main sentence.]

We have dedicated staff across all the campuses to guide you through the process and help you make the right choice; so, it doesn't matter where you're based. You will be given a basic induction, so you know what is expected of you and what support you can expect from us. [Unravel the long and rambling sentence by creating two sentences and inserting some punctuation; remove 'for you' as redundant.] Your expenses will be covered, so volunteering won't cost you anything. [Insert a comma between the clauses for clarity.] Volunteering is a two-way process, in which volunteers gain as much from their experience as the people they work with. [Insert hyphen in 'two-way'; insert comma and change relative pronoun for the non-defining relative clause.]

It is crucial to find a volunteering opportunity that matches your skills and interests. Therefore, we have a continually expanding range of opportunities available with various charities and organisations. [Remove comma and change relative pronoun for the defining relative clause; split the sentence, so that 'therefore', followed by a comma, begins a second sentence.] Don't worry, we'll help you pick the right placement for you, to fit in with your needs and your schedule; and so you get the most out of it! [Correct 'you're' to 'your'; add 'and' and semicolon before the final clause.] If we don't currently offer something that you really want, we will do our best to find something for you. [Insert comma after the *if* clause for clarity.]

8 Why Can't I Rely on My Computer's Grammar checker?

If you use Microsoft Word as your word processing program, and most of us do, then you will be aware that it has a spelling and grammar checking facility. Indeed, the program usually comes with the facility already activated, so you will be familiar with the red and green wavy underlining – red for a spelling offence and green for a grammar one; though, if you're one of the ten per cent of males that are red/green colour-blind (like me), you'll have difficulty telling the difference. When the wavy lines begin to annoy you, you'll want to turn the facility off. After much searching in Word's menus, you will finally come across it and discover that the grammar-checking part is actually quite complex. This chapter looks at Word's grammar checker and asks if you can trust it.

Finding the Grammar Checker

If you've never found the grammar checker before, follow these steps (you need to have a document open in Word):

- Enter the 'Tools' menu ('Spelling & Grammar ...' at the top of the menu is the instruction to conduct a check on the document you have open, so ignore it).
- Select 'Options ...' at the bottom of the menu.
- Select the tab labelled 'Spelling & Grammar'.

Down the left-hand side of the 'Spelling & Grammar' options is a series of boxes that you can insert ticks into or remove ticks from, by clicking on the box with your mouse. This is how you turn the check-as-you-go facility on and off. Towards the bottom on the right, you will see a box that is headed 'Writing style'. If you click on the arrow to the right of the box, you will be presented with a number of options: Casual, Standard, Formal, Technical, Custom. The preset option is usually 'standard'. These represent a variety of 'writing styles', for each of which Word has a different set of items that it checks.

To see what these items are, click on the button just below the 'Writing style' box, marked 'Settings …'. This opens up a further window, headed 'Grammar Settings'. At the top is a 'Writing style' box, in which you can select a writing style. In the larger box below is a set of options: the first three relate to punctuation checks that you can ask the checker to perform; then there is a series of thirteen grammar checks, some of which are to do with spelling and punctuation rather than grammar; and finally there is a set of thirteen style checks. To see which ones are turned on for a particular 'writing style', select a writing style in the top box. The 'casual' style has only five grammar checks and no style ones; the 'standard' style has all but two of the grammar checks and none of the style checks; the 'formal' style has all the grammar checks and all but two of the style checks; and the 'technical' style has all but two of the grammar checks and seven of the style checks. The 'custom' style ticks all the boxes, except the 'Use of first person' under style. This writing style option enables you to select which checks you personally want turned on. Click on a ticked box to remove the tick; a further click will restore the tick.

The major difficulty in designing your own, customised grammar/style checker is in understanding exactly what is meant by some of the items listed. The label 'Negation' or 'Relative clauses', for example, doesn't inform us what aspects of negation or relative clauses are to be checked. The label 'Sentence structure' doesn't enlighten us at all, nor does 'Verb and noun phrases' or 'Unclear phrasing' or 'Wordiness'. There must be some checking routines underlying these labels, but they remain opaque to the user, and the query facility (the question mark in the top right-hand corner) does not provide any help.

The grammar checker in Word concentrates on a limited number of items, pre-selected for a particular 'writing style' – the 'standard' one, unless otherwise specified. In order to perform the check, the grammar checker must undertake a grammatical analysis of the sentence under scrutiny (and it is all sentence-based). The grammatical analysis must be accurate for any advice that is given to be valid, since the advice is, inevitably, based on the analysis. So, if the grammar checker performs an inaccurate analysis, the advice is invalid; but that is something that you, as a user, cannot necessarily judge. The grammar of English is a highly complex and open-ended mechanism, in which words may have multiple functions and constructions may have a number of possible variations. A computer program that will successfully cope with all the possible variation in English grammar would be enormous and highly sophisticated, and it has probably yet to be written. But, let's try this one out!

Using the Grammar Checker

I subjected a draft of Chapter 6 of this book to Word's grammar checker, using the 'formal' writing style, which I considered to be the appropriate one for an academic textbook, even though I have adopted a fairly informal tone. I, or the writers I have quoted in that chapter, offended against the grammar checker on well in excess of fifty occasions. Here is a flavour of some of the errors that it noted or the advice that it proffered.

It consistently objected when I failed to insert a comma after an initial prepositional phrase or conjunctive adverb. For example, I wrote:

In the previous chapter we looked at ...

The grammar checker wanted:

In the previous chapter, we looked at ...

I wrote:

In a developing narrative the initial sentence ...

The grammar checker wanted:

In a developing narrative, the initial sentence ...

I quoted:

> Yet the equity orientation of ...
> Moreover the entry of the UK ...

The grammar checker wanted:

> Yet, the equity orientation of ...
> Moreover, the entry of the UK ...

It may be in the interests of clarity and readability for a comma to occur in this position, but it is, in the end, a matter of the writer's judgment whether a comma is needed on any particular occasion. A computer program does not have that judgment: it must decide either 'yes' or 'no', and this one is programmed to say 'yes'.

The grammar checker consistently queried passive constructions and advised: 'consider revising'. There were dozens of these in the chapter, for example:

> ... sentences could be rearranged ...
> ... the paragraph division is justified ...

In most instances an active version of the sentence would have been more wordy and less comprehensible. To avoid such querying by the grammar checker, the 'technical' writing style would have to be selected. In most cases, the grammar checker correctly analysed passive constructions, though it cannot always distinguish between genuine passives and '*be* + past participle as adjective' constructions. Arguably, the second example above is of this kind: this is not based on 'someone justifies the paragraph division' but is, rather, parallel to 'the paragraph division is reasonable'. The proscription of passive sentences is based on a particular view of 'good style'; yet, interestingly, it occurs in the 'grammar' list and not the 'style' list.

The grammar checker objected to the use of *and* or *but* at the beginning of a sentence. I wrote:

> But it is arguable ...
> And there was the ...

The grammar checker suggested rewording *But* with either *However* or *Nevertheless*, and *And* with either *In addition* or *Moreover*, all followed, of course, by a comma. Again, as we argued in that chapter, a blanket proscription against initial *but* or *and* deprives a writer of the stylistic nuances that can be achieved by judicious use of an initial co-ordinating conjunction.

I offended against the 'long sentence' rule (more than sixty words) on one occasion, with a sentence of sixty-one words. The grammar checker also objected to my (or others') use of what it considered convoluted phrasing. It wanted to replace 'bring the episode to a conclusion' with 'conclude the episode', and 'it goes without saying' with 'it is understood', and 'on the grounds that' with *because*. It accused me of 'wordiness' with the expression 'perhaps not so unusual'; and it didn't like the 'order of words' in 'the conjunctive adverb may, however, occur within ... .' It didn't like the 'beginning of sentence' in 'But the confusion of identity is the precise target of Stoppard's humour ...', though it wasn't any more precise on the reason for its disliking. It objected, understandably within a formal style, to contractions like *can't* and *he'd*. The grammar checker's judgments are not always transparent, and it is not always the case that its suggestions improve the style of the writing that it is trying to correct.

The grammar checker has a fundamental problem with relative clauses, and some extremely rigid rules. For example, I quoted:

I wrote about a Japanese couple who visited their ...

The grammar checker demanded:

I wrote about a Japanese couple that visited their ...

I quoted:

The seaweed which is cultivated on them ...

The grammar checker wanted either:

The seaweed that is cultivated on them ...

or:

> The seaweed, which is cultivated on them, ...

The rules for relative clauses that (or which) are programmed into the grammar checker follow those of some rather strict copyeditors: if the relative clause is defining, and is therefore not surrounded by commas, then the relative pronoun must be *that*; *who* and *which* are used only for non-defining relative clauses. This is pedantic in the extreme, and the practice is rarely followed by writers these days.

There was one further interesting suggestion in respect of relative clauses: in the following

> Another police source, who did not want ...

The grammar checker advised to use *which*, rather than *who*. Presumably, it had analysed *source* as non-personal, whereas in this particular instance it relates to a personal referent, *police source*.

The grammar checker does not like hyphens! It wanted *home-made* written solid, *homemade*; but it wanted *well-stocked* written open, *well stocked*. Similarly, it asked for *sea-lettuce* to be written *sea lettuce*; but this compound noun was in the noun phrase *green sea-lettuce*. If you remove the hyphen (*green sea lettuce*), it becomes ambiguous whether *green* relates to *sea* or to *lettuce*. In this analysis, the grammar checker was unable to investigate the context beyond the compound noun.

Sometimes the grammar checker performs an inaccurate analysis and so makes inappropriate suggestions. For example, it pointed up the following as a 'fragment', by which it meant a verbless sentence:

> Whether funding mosques will lead to better relations with Muslim immigrants remains to be seen.

The grammar checker has, clearly, not recognised *remains* as the main verb in this sentence; it appears to have analysed the whole of it as a subordinate clause introduced by *whether*, without recognising that the *whether* clause is the subject of *remains*. Similarly, in:

> ... the image the BBC projects is extremely important ...

The grammar checker suggests that it should be *projects are* or *project is*. It analyses *projects* as a noun, and not as the verb that it is. It doesn't recognise that the subject of *is* is the noun *image* and that *the BBC projects* is a relative clause with omitted relative pronoun (*which/that*). Relative clauses that have no introductory relative pronoun are hard to detect. In the following:

> ... produce a consistent style, neither overly Germanic, nor slav-ishly following the New World cult ...

The grammar checker wants *overly neither*, instead of *neither overly*. Here it seems to be analysing *Germanic* as a noun (because there is no noun following – it's in fact *style*), and so *overly*, as an adverb, is not an appro-priate modifier for the supposed noun. The grammar checker also mis-interpreted the contraction *he'd*, cited earlier: it wanted to replace it by *he would*, whereas in the context it should have been *he had*.

Arguably, this is the most serious problem with the grammar checker: its analysis program is not sufficiently powerful and sophisticated to deal with some of the subtleties of English grammar, and so it offers inappro-priate, or even plain wrong, advice. How is the (grammatically naïve) user to know? The grammar checker had another problem with Chapter 6: it was unable to perceive when I was citing words or phrases (usually those in italics), and so it analysed them as if they were being used normally. Inevitably, it detected a number of errors that weren't there.

What's my advice? Turn your grammar checker off and forget about it. It is as likely to mislead as to provide useful advice. Instead, learn some-thing about grammar, its wonderful complexity and sophistication; and, on the basis of what you have learned and know, make your own judg-ments about the suitability of your sentence constructions for your text and its audience.

Is the Spellchecker Any Better?

The program behind the spellchecker is, inevitably, much simpler. It has to check each word – identified by the spaces and/or punctuation that surround it – against those stored in its dictionary. It does this using a sophisticated search algorithm that speeds up the process. It also allows you to create your own dictionary of words that you use regularly but which are not in its standard dictionary; and when it checks it will search against both lists. You can usually also select whether you wish the check to be carried out against American English spelling or British English spelling.

The spellchecker will query any word that is not in its (or your) dictionary, and usually it will offer one or more suggestions to enable you to correct the misspelling. For example, if you type *acommodation*, it will put the wavy red line underneath, and it will suggest that you really meant to type *accommodation*. It will perform similarly with *begining, chocalate, extrordinary, messanger*, and many other common misspellings.

However, if you mistype a word and in the process create a word that is stored in its dictionary, then the spellchecker will not query it. If, for example, you type *form* and you meant to type *from*, the spellchecker will not be able to tell you – and reversing the order of letters is a common typing mistake. Similarly, the spellchecker will not alert you if you have used *affect* instead of *effect*, or *principle* instead of *principal*. It won't help you to sort out *there, their* and *they're*, or *your* and *you're*. Neither will it query your use of *lead* as the past tense of *lead*, instead of *led*. All these are common mistakes, and the spellchecker cannot come to your aid.

What's my advice? It is worth running your text through the spellchecker, or keeping the check-as-you-go facility switched on. This will pick up some of your misspellings, and, unlike the grammar checker, it will not give you confusing or misleading advice. But do not think that, having run your text through the spellchecker, it is now perfectly spelled. It will still need proofreading. And if there are cases where you are unsure – if it should be *lead* or *led*, for example – then you will need to look the word up (see further Chapter 9).

Some Practical Tips

Are you one of those students who, once they have completed a piece of work, cannot bear to look at it again? Steel yourself! Any writer must be prepared to look over their work and to revise it. Make sure that you leave yourself time to do this. Checking your work is best done not immediately after you have finished it. You are more likely to notice mistakes and to make sensible judgments about how you have phrased something, if you come back to it afresh after a day or so. This requires some organisation on your part, so that you are not typing the final paragraph just as the final deadline for handing in looms. Aim to finish a piece of coursework at least two or three days before it is due in. Then you leave yourself time for checking and revision.

After twenty-four hours or so have elapsed, go back to your piece of writing. Read it through, if possible out loud. Be prepared to revise any clumsy or unclear expression, and to make connections more explicit, if that is required. If you are unsure about something, a spelling or a grammatical construction, take time to look it up (see Chapter 10).

More generally, develop your intuitions and feeling for language. Learn more about English grammar: this book has been able to introduce you to only the basics. Be aware of language usage: read critically the texts that you encounter on a daily basis. As a student, language is your basic tool in persuading others of your learning, achievements and worth. It will repay spending some time developing your ability to use language; it does not come automatically, especially as far as written language in the more formal registers is concerned. If you make an effort to develop your linguistic abilities and language awareness, then both the task of setting down your thoughts in the first place and the chore of checking and revising your work will become easier.

EXERCISE

Take a recent piece of your own writing and submit it to MS Word's spellchecker and grammar checker. How does it fare? Did it produce any useful advice, any confusing advice, any plain wrong advice?

9 Spelling and Punctuation

While neither spelling nor punctuation belongs strictly speaking to what linguists regard as grammar, they are important aspects of written communication. It is, therefore, appropriate to consider them in the context of a book like this, especially since they are features of writing that many readers notice most readily, and they are the subject of much controversy.

Spelling

Spelling is the most standardised feature of the English language. The spelling of English words has changed little since the eighteenth century; and, whatever accent you may have, you are expected to spell in the same way as everyone else. Because pronunciation has undergone a number of changes over the centuries and there is no 'standard' pronunciation, the relation between the pronunciation and spelling of words has grown wider. Just consider how the letter sequence 'ough' is pronounced in the following: *through, rough, cough, bought, sough*. But the sound in *through* is represented by 'oo' in *too*, that in *rough* by 'uff' in *cuff*, that in *cough* by 'of' in *soft*, that in *bought* by 'or' in *sort*, and that in *sough* by 'ow' in *cow*. This is just one illustration of the mismatch between sound and letter in English. We are using a medieval spelling to represent twenty-first century pronunciation.

Yet, since the eighteenth century, correct spelling has become a prime indicator of an educated person. A relationship is drawn, not least by some secretaries of state for education, between good spelling and good character. When employers complain, as they have done for decades, about the levels of literacy of their new recruits, spelling is at the forefront of their minds. If your text is littered with misspellings, it makes a bad impression, and as a result your reader may query your intellectual competence. It is one of those things that can get in the way of the effective communication of your message. Pedantic and unfair as it may be, this is the way things are. So, if you are a poor speller, this is something worth working on.

Despite the standardised nature of English spelling, there are two ways in which spellings may legitimately vary. First, there are the differences between American English (AmE) and British English (BrE) spellings, as a consequence of the spelling reforms initiated by the nineteenth century American lexicographer, Noah Webster. The main differences are:

- AmE *-er*   for BrE *-re*   in words like *center, theater*
- AmE *-or*   for BrE *-our*   in words like *color, flavor*
- AmE *-e-*   for BrE *-ae-*   in words like *anemic, medieval*
- AmE *-se*   for BrE *-ce*   in words like *defense, offense*
- AmE *-ize*   for BrE *-ise*   in words like *realize, traumatize*
- dropping a vowel letter(s) in words like *ax, story* (for *storey*), *catalog*
- keeping a single consonant before a suffix in words like *traveling*.

Most of these are considered unacceptable in British English, except that both *-ize* and *-ise* spellings are found, and dictionaries usually list the *-ize* spelling as the preferred one. If writing for publication, you should check which the publisher requires. Also, British English is beginning to adopt the *e* for *ae* spelling in words like *archeology, encyclopedia, medieval*.

The other kind of variation is the simple fact that quite a number of words have alternative spellings, both of which are accepted as standard:

adviser	advisor	bandolier	bandoleer
crummy	crumby	dexterous	dextrous
embed	imbed	fetid	foetid
gelatin	gelatine	hiccup	hiccough
immovable	immoveable	judgment	judgement
kilogram	kilogramme	leitmotif	leitmotiv
mortise	mortice	nosy	nosey
ostler	hostler	pedlar	peddler
quartet	quartette	repellent	repellant
sari	saree	T-shirt	tee shirt

veranda	verandah	wych elm	witch elm
yogurt	yoghourt	Zion	Sion

This is a selection, culled from the *Concise Oxford Dictionary* (1999); there are probably several thousand words that have alternative spellings. This does not make it any easier to get spelling right.

There are two areas where most spelling mistakes occur. The first is with homophones – words that are pronounced the same, but which are spelt (spelled) differently; or with words that sound very similar. Here are some of the most frequently confused pairs:

accept	except	adapt	adopt
adverse	averse	affect	effect
amoral	immoral	bail	bale
breach	breech	broach	brooch
canvas	canvass	climatic	climactic
coarse	course	dependant	dependent
dialectal	dialectical	discreet	discrete
diverse	divers	draft	draught
dual	duel	elicit	illicit
emotional	emotive	envelop	envelope
flaunt	flout	hoard	horde
imminent	immanent	ingenious	ingenuous
lead	led	licence	license
lose	loose	luxuriant	luxurious
maybe	may be	militate	mitigate
perquisite	pre-requisite	persecute	prosecute
pore	pour	practice	practise
precede	proceed	prescribe	proscribe
principal	principle	rack	wrack
sensual	sensuous	stationary	stationery
stimulant	stimulus	systematic	systemic
there	their	their	they're
to too	two	troop	troupe
venal	venial	vicious	viscous

If you are uncertain about any of these often confused pairs of words, you should look them up, in for example, R.L. Trask's *Mind the Gaffe*

(Penguin 2001), from which they were culled and which contains much useful advice.

The second area where spelling mistakes commonly occur is when a suffix is added to a word and a spelling change takes place, though usually not without exception. There are three main changes and one minor that take place when a suffix is added to a word.

1 A final -e is deleted if the suffix begins with a vowel:

hope + -ing	=	hoping
hope + -ed	=	hoped
serve + -ice	=	service
moisture + -ize	=	moisturize
collapse + -ible	=	collapsible

With the -able suffix, however, there is some variation:

love + -able	=	lovable
like + -able	=	likeable

But *loveable* and *likable* are also possible; compare *movable/ moveable, unshakeable/unshakable*.

2 A final consonant preceded by a short vowel doubles before a suffix beginning with a vowel:

step + -ing	=	stepping (but not in *steeping*)
step + -ed	=	stepped (or in *steeped*)
begin + -ing	=	beginning
pot + -ery	=	pottery
regret + -able	=	regrettable
mad + -er	=	madder

This is not without exception:

gallop + -ing	=	galloping
benefit + -ed	=	benefited (but also *benefitted*)

3 A final -y changes to -i when a suffix is added:

fly + -s	=	flies
dry + -er	=	drier

carry + -age	=	carriage
deny + -al	=	denial
silly + -ness	=	silliness
accompany + -ment	=	accompaniment

The exception is before -ing, where the potential double 'ii' keeps the -y:

carry + -ing	=	carrying
try + -ing	=	trying

There are one or two other exceptions: *dryer* is usual for a 'machine that dries washing'; *fryer* for a 'receptacle for frying'; *slyly*, but also *slily*; *dryness* but *drily*.

4   **A fourth and rather minor change is the addition of a 'k' when a word ends in -c and the suffixes -ing or -ed are added:**

frolic	frolicking	frolicked
picnic	picnicking	picnicked
traffic	trafficking	trafficked

We all have trouble remembering the spelling of some words, and we need to continually remind ourselves of the correct spelling.

EXERCISE

Is the correct spelling

accomodation	or	accommodation?
beleive	or	believe?
committment	or	commitment?
critisise	or	criticise?
definately	or	definitely?
dissappear	or	disappear?
freind	or	friend?
medecine	or	medicine?

neccesary	or	necessary?
ocassion	or	occasion?
occurence	or	occurrence?
tommorrow	or	tomorrow?

In fact, in all these cases, the correct spelling is the one on the right. If you are unsure, there is nothing for it but to keep checking.

What is my advice? First of all, don't be so cocksure that your spelling of a word is necessarily right: have a little linguistic humility. Then, have a routine for checking the spelling of a word that you are not sure of. Either keep a print dictionary to hand, or, more conveniently, have a dictionary on your computer (CD-ROM versions of dictionaries, which can be loaded onto your hard drive, are no more expensive than their print versions). If in doubt, look it up!

Punctuation

An email (or e-mail) sent by a students union president to senior academic staff in his university contained the following 'sentence':

> Just wanted to let you know that I'm convening the Union of Students induction talks for the new freshers this year and wanted to offer the opportunity to all faculties to book us if you require us to do a talk to any of your courses we are more than happy to if you can let me know via the contact details below asap it would be much appreciated.

Now, even for email English, this is rather lacking in punctuation, and you need to read it a couple of times to realise how the clauses relate to each other. I'd suggest the following as rather more helpful to his readers:

> Just wanted to let you know that I'm convening the Union of Students induction talks for the new freshers this year and wanted to offer the opportunity to all faculties to book us. If you require us to do a talk to any of your courses, we are more than happy to. If

you can let me know via the contact details below asap, it would be much appreciated.

Some might want to suggest even more punctuation:

> Just wanted to let you know that I'm convening the Union of Students induction talks for the new freshers this year, and wanted to offer the opportunity to all faculties to book us. If you require us to do a talk to any of your courses, we are more than happy to. If you can let me know, via the contact details below, asap, it would be much appreciated.

Punctuation is a mechanism of writing; it is not useful to regard it as in any way related to speech. You should forget about any rules of the kind: 'put a comma where you would pause in speech'. They don't work. The purpose of punctuation is to enable your reader to interpret unambiguously the structure, and therefore the meaning, of your writing. The absence of full stops to distinguish the sentences in the email above is, in effect, an insult to the readers. It tells the readers to work it out for themselves. Poorly punctuated writing can make for frustrated and annoyed readers, who will be less sympathetic to appreciating the content of what you are writing. So, punctuation is important.

The punctuation marks used in English writing are the following:

- **ending sentences: full stop [.], question mark [?], exclamation mark [!]**
- **within sentences: comma [,], semicolon [;], colon [:]**
- **within words: apostrophe ['], hyphen [-]**
- **for parenthesis: brackets [()], dash [—]**
- **for quotation: single quotation marks ['...'], double quotation marks ["..."].**

Though not strictly punctuation, the use of capital letters is also a feature of writing that has no counterpart in speech.

Let us now examine, in broad outline, how these features are used. Before we do so, it should be said that, while there are some very clear rules of punctuation, there is also much about punctuation that is at the discretion of the individual writer. Punctuation practice has varied over the centuries, with eighteenth century texts, for example, being much more heavily punctuated than is the usual practice today. The focus of this discussion is on enabling you to help your reader to navigate their way through your text.

ENDING SENTENCES

These are the most straightforward of the punctuation marks to use. One of them should terminate a grammatical sentence (though see on the colon and semicolon below). Avoid run-on sentences (see Chapter 7). Question marks should be used only with direct questions:

What are the rules for punctuation?

and not with indirect questions, since these are reporting (= a statement) a question:

The student asked what the rules for punctuation were.

You should rarely need to use the exclamation mark in academic writing. Its usual function is to reinforce a direct imperative:

Write on one side of the paper only!

or to signal an exclamative outburst:

What a marvellous view you have from your window!

Such sentences would be extremely unusual in academic essays and reports. I might have been tempted to use an exclamation mark at the end of the previous sentence, but I resisted. Incidentally, there is no space between the last letter of the last word of a sentence and the punctuation mark.

WITHIN SENTENCES

This is where punctuation begins to get tricky, but the general principle is that, within a sentence, punctuation should make explicit the grammatical structure of the sentence. It should show which words belong together in a grammatical structure, a phrase or a clause. Consider the following example:

> A wide range of human activities can trigger or exacerbate land degradation; there are also environments which are very vulnerable to degradation, and natural catastrophes from time to time degrade virtually all environments. (FLOB J03)

This sentence contains three clauses. The first is divided from the second and third by a semicolon, and the second is divided from the third by a comma. Since the semicolon is a 'stronger' or 'heavier' punctuation mark than the comma, the author wishes us to understand that the second and third clauses are more closely related to each other than is the first to either of them. This is a good illustration of how punctuation is being used to guide the reader in interpreting the text.

Note, however, in the example above that the comma precedes a conjunction, in this case *and*. Without the conjunction, it would be an example of a run-on sentence. Normally, a comma is used to divide clauses within a sentence where the subject of the clauses is different, and a conjunction is being used. Also with a dividing function is the comma that separates an initial adverbial (adverb, prepositional phrase, or adverbial clause) from the rest of the sentence:

> Commonly, a chain-of-causation stretches away in space and/or time from the site where land degradation is manifest. (FLOB J03)

> In the short term, these events cause degradation ... (FLOB J03)

> ... instead of exciting a nucleon, the incident particle excites a collective mode ... (FLOB J01)

Whether a comma is needed in this position is a matter of judgment. It is insisted on by Microsoft Word's grammar checker (Chapter 8), but you will need to judge whether your sentence is made clearer by introducing a comma in this position. Note, however, that a comma separating the subject of the sentence from the rest creates only confusion and is unnecessary:

His momentary lapse of attention, caused the accident.

The comma is also used to separate items in a list, for example of adjectives modifying a noun:

The wide-ranging, large-leaved, evergreen, tropical and paratropical rain forests of the Eocene had contracted ... (FLOB J04)

Notice that the last adjective in the list, *paratropical*, is joined to the others by *and*, which is not preceded by a comma. A comma is not needed at this point, though practice seems to vary, especially where a list is very long:

... and a few are even bringing world-class teaching expertise in subjects such as sports, gymnastics, singing, ballet, circus, and mathematics. (FLOB J36)

The other main use of the comma is for parenthesis, or bracketing; we will consider this use below, along with brackets and dashes.

The third within-sentence punctuation mark is the colon. It is normally preceded by a complete sentence, but what follows may range from a single word to a complete sentence. The element on the right of the colon usually functions as an illustration or explanation of what is on the left:

From the Hamiltonian viewpoint, these pairs have a curious feature: one of the flows in question takes place on a (slightly degenerate) symplectic manifold, the other on a Poisson manifold. (FLOB J21)

What comes after the colon explains the 'curious feature'.

Continuous resources include: solar energy, wind, gravity, tidal energy, geothermal energy. (FLOB J03)

The colon introduces a list of 'continuous resources'. The colon is sometimes used to introduce a direct quotation, but this is not necessary:

Bleich notes: 'If there is no external standard, collective interests are the highest authority.' (FLOB J62)

A comma would serve equally well here, but, note, not a semicolon.

WITHIN WORDS

This is the area of punctuation in which there is most confusion: the apostrophe and the hyphen. The apostrophe is used for essentially two purposes: to indicate 'possession' and to signal omitted letters. The possession function relates to nouns. Compare the following forms:

girl	girl's	girls'
woman	woman's	women's
witness	witness's	witnesses'

The items in the first column are the base, uninflected forms of the noun; those in the second are the singular noun inflected for possession; and those in the third are the plural noun inflected for possession. You will note that where the plural is formed irregularly (*women*), the -'*s* is used, rather than the usual -*s*. With names that end in 's' or 'z', there is some variation as to whether -'*s* is added for the possessive or simply an apostrophe:

James's	or	James'
Socrates's	or	Socrates'
Jesus's	or	Jesus'

The deciding factor is what it sounds like: *James's* sounds all right, but *Socrates'* and *Jesus'* are preferred to their alternatives.

The use of the apostrophe to signal omitted letters is most widespread in verb phrase contractions, either auxiliary plus *not* contractions:

isn't, aren't, wasn't, weren't, hasn't, haven't, hadn't, doesn't, don't, didn't, can't, couldn't, won't (will + not), wouldn't, shan't (shall + not), shouldn't, mustn't, mayn't, mightn't

or pronoun plus auxiliary contractions:

I'm, we're, you're, they're, she's (=she + is and she + has), he's (similarly), it's (similarly), I've, we've, you've, they've, I'd

(= I + had and I + would), we'd (similarly), you'd (similarly), they'd (similarly), she'd (similarly), I'll, we'll, you'll, they'll, he'll, it'll.

Some points to be underlined here are:

- the contraction of *you are* is *you're* (not *your*)
- the contraction of *they are* is *they're* (not *their* and definitely not *there*)
- *it's* is only ever a contraction, of *it is* or *it has* (the possessive is *its*, without an apostrophe)
- *it's* is like *she's* and *he's*, a contraction; *its* is like *her(s)* and *his*, a possessive.

Because the confusion of *it's* and *its* is so widespread – I have seen the wrong one used in a university vice-chancellor's email – it could be triggering a change in linguistic usage. For now, though, the distinction should be maintained, if only for the sake of consistency and to avoid confusion: if *it's* were accepted as a possessive (determiner or pronoun), then it would be the only one in the series with an apostrophe. Compare:

my, your, his, her, its, our, their; mine, yours, his, hers, its, ours, theirs

which is the accepted (correct) series, with:

my, your, his, her, it's, our, their; mine, yours, his, hers, it's, ours, theirs

in which it stands out as odd.

The omitted letter use of the apostrophe was also used where words had been abbreviated:

'bus (for *omnibus*), 'fridge (originally spelt *'frig*, for *refrigerator*), 'phone (for *telephone*).

This practice is archaic and no longer followed. Going the same way is the use of the apostrophe for the plurals of decades and acronyms:

1960s, 1960's; TVs, TV's.

The form without apostrophe is now the preferred one. This practice spawned the so-called 'greengrocer's apostrophe' in plurals like *tomato's* and *potato's*, which spread to the electrical store's *video's* and *hi-fi's*. In none of these cases is an apostrophe appropriate.

The other within-word punctuation mark is the hyphen, used to mark a compound word or to attach a prefix where there might be ambiguity about how to pronounce it:

> bus-driver, by-election, city-wide, closely-guarded, ex-patients, sun-drenched, good-looking, inner-city, life-style, off-licence, push-chair, co-operate.

The trend these days is not to use the hyphen. Consequently, compounds are written either solid (*lifestyle, pushchair*) or open (*bus driver, closely guarded*). The hyphen is being left out of *co-operate* (so *cooperate*), and from *ex-patients* (but as *ex patients*). This is resulting in prefixes becoming stranded: *Pro Vice Chancellor* is now usual, as against *Pro-Vice-Chancellor*. A number of prefixes have traditionally been attached by a hyphen, for example:

> co-, ex-, non-, post-, pro-, pseudo-, self-, semi-.

The trend seems to be for the hyphen to be omitted and the prefix to stand alone and unattached.

Clearly, the use of the hyphen is an area of the language undergoing change, and usage is currently highly variable. A good example of this variability is the use of the adverb *well* before a past participle as adjective (*well-established, well-known*). Traditionally, it has been attached to the adjective by a hyphen; but usage is currently tending towards a preference for no hyphen (*well established, well known*). My advice is to use an up-to-date dictionary and to stick with its recommendations; or if writing for publication, check on the publisher's house style.

PARENTHESIS

A phrase or clause may be indicated as parenthetical, or as an aside, by three different means of punctuation: commas, brackets, and dashes.

If population grows, but not too fast, then intensive agriculture, possibly causing less land degradation, may result. (FLOB J03)

The basic structure of this sentence is:

If population grows, then intensive agriculture may result.

Two parenthetical comments have been inserted, bracketed by commas:

but not too fast
possibly causing less land degradation.

Here is an example with brackets:

Cannel coal (dull with conchoidal fracture) represents drifted, finely-divided terrestrial plant material. (FLOB J02)

And now an example with dashes:

Some of these – perhaps the first four – might seem to be the common property of all readers. (FLOB J60)

The use of commas round a non-defining relative clause (Chapters 4, 7) falls into this category, with the relative clause as an extra piece of information about a noun.

QUOTATION

Double quotation marks may be used for direct quotation:

"I do not admit", said Palmerston, "that our policy has been a selfish one in the sense in which the word is sometimes employed." (FLOB J57)

The National Health Service Act 1977 creates a duty to provide services for the diagnosis and treatment of illness (section 3) and defines "illness" as "any injury or disability requiring medical or dental treatment or nursing" (section 128). (FLOB J50)

Single quotation marks may be used where a writer wishes to distance themselves from the import or meaning of the item within the quotation marks; it is the equivalent of using *so-called*:

> Should such practice be regarded as 'negligent' and hence subject to legal pressures, or should there be a voluntary code of practice? (FLOB J13)

> As a consequence of this market-driven production philosophy, firms must also take on new organizational structures such as the 'flat organization' or 'polycentricism'. (FLOB J44)

However, the uses are more-or-less interchangeable. Another use of single quotation marks is as an alternative to using italics when you are citing (talking about) a word:

> ... Behn's use of the first person plural, which is not the authorial 'we' and contrasts sharply with the narrator's jauntily individualistic 'I' ... (FLOB J63)

> The term 'speech act' refers to an utterance which not only articulates, but actually brings into being a particular state of affairs. (FLOB J61)

Publishers usually have a system of single outer, double inner quotation marks (as in this book), or vice versa.

CAPITAL LETTERS

Capital letters are used for the first letter of a sentence:

> How can these be reassembled as a reconstruction of the original plant? (FLOB J02)

They are also used for the initial letter of: proper names, days of the week, months of the year, countries and languages, peoples and religious affiliations, festivals, institutions, offices, and titles of books, films etc:

> Henry Higgins, Tuesday, September, Hungary, German, Berbers, Taoists, Easter, House of Commons, President Chirac, *The Hound of the Baskervilles*.

Most acronyms and initialisms are also written with capital letters:

BBC, CD-ROM, DVD, LAN, UNESCO.

There are some instances where the usage is variable, and there is a tendency not to use capital letters unless really necessary, for example with words like *university, faculty, department*. A distinction is sometimes drawn between a general reference and the title of a specific entity:

Each faculty should have a five-year plan.
You should enquire in the Faculty of Law.

This has given an overview of spelling and punctuation. You can follow these points up in the references given in Chapter 10.

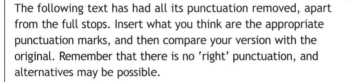

EXERCISE

The following text has had all its punctuation removed, apart from the full stops. Insert what you think are the appropriate punctuation marks, and then compare your version with the original. Remember that there is no 'right' punctuation, and alternatives may be possible.

Scientists with the best of motives can produce bad science just as scientists whose motives may be considered suspect can produce good science. An obvious example of the first was Rachel Carson who if not the patron saint was at least the founding mother of modern environmentalism. Her book *The Silent Spring* was an inspiring account of the damage caused to our natural environment by the reckless spraying of pesticides especially DDT.

However Carson also claimed that DDT caused cancer and liver damage claims for which there is no evidence but which led to an effective worldwide ban on the use of DDT that is proving disastrous. Her motives were pure the science was wrong. DDT is the most effective agent ever invented for preventing insect-borne disease which according to the US National Academy of Sciences and the WHO prevented over 50 million human deaths from malaria in about two decades. Although there is no evidence that DDT harms human health some NGOs still demand a worldwide ban for that reason. Careless science cost lives.

(From *Education Guardian* website education.guardian.co.uk, 21 February 2005.)

Now, here is the original version:

Scientists with the best of motives can produce bad science, just as scientists whose motives may be considered suspect can produce good science. An obvious example of the first was Rachel Carson, who, if not the patron saint, was at least the founding mother of modern environmentalism. Her book *The Silent Spring* was an inspiring account of the damage caused to our natural environment by the reckless spraying of pesticides, especially DDT.

However, Carson also claimed that DDT caused cancer and liver damage, claims for which there is no evidence but which led to an effective worldwide ban on the use of DDT that is proving disastrous. Her motives were pure; the science was wrong. DDT is the most effective agent ever invented for preventing insect-borne disease, which, according to the US National Academy of Sciences and the WHO, prevented over 50 million human deaths from malaria in about two decades. Although there is no evidence that DDT harms human health, some NGOs still demand a worldwide ban for that reason. Careless science cost lives.

Can you see how the punctuation aids the reader to navigate the text more easily, and in some instances is essential for this purpose?

10 Where To Go for Further Information

This small book has been able to give you but an introduction to the resources of English grammar, and only a small selection of tips and advice for writing effective essays and reports. What it has emphasised is that the resources of language are there for you to exploit; and that the more you know about the English language and how it works, the better prepared you will be to exploit effectively its resources. To do this, you need to know where to look for information and advice about linguistic usage. This chapter points you in the direction of some useful sources, in both print and electronic media.

Grammars

One of the most accessible and lucid, as well as prolific, writers on the English language is David Crystal. His highly regarded book on English grammar was published in a new edition in 2004, along with a companion volume:

Rediscover Grammar, ISBN 0582848628
Making Sense of Grammar, ISBN 0582848636.

Both books are published by Longman (Pearson Education). The first one explores the structures and mechanisms of grammar, while the second examines how grammar works in different contexts of use and in various types of text.

The most up-to-date reference grammar of English is the:

Longman Grammar of Spoken and Written English, ISBN 0582237254.

It was compiled by a team of linguists from Europe and America: Douglas Biber, Stig Johansson, Geoffrey Leech, Susan Conrad, Edward Finegan. It has over 1200 pages and was published in 1999. This grammar is based on the analysis of a large computer corpus of English texts, and it is, thus, able to give reliable information about the frequency and distribution of grammatical features and patterns in different types of text and discourse.

An abbreviated, 'student' version of this grammar was published in 2002, written by Douglas Biber, Geoffrey Leech and Susan Conrad, under the title:

Longman Student Grammar of Spoken and Written English, ISBN 0582237262 (paperback edition).

Another corpus-based, and more conveniently sized reference grammar is the:

Collins COBUILD English Grammar, ISBN 000370257X.

This grammar was developed by the COBUILD team at the University of Birmingham, under the direction of John Sinclair. It is characterised by copious examples from the COBUILD corpus. The grammar was originally published in 1990, and it is aimed primarily at advanced students and teachers of English. It can usefully be used, though, by anyone needing a reference grammar.

Grammars of English abound. They come in varying sizes, aimed at different audiences – foreign learners, school students, journalists – and of varying quality and reliability. Those mentioned above are recommended as accurate and reliable, as well as presenting their information in an accessible form.

A similarly reliable grammar is to be found on the internet. The *Internet Grammar of English* has been developed by a team at University College London, and it is located on UCL's website:

http://www.ucl.ac.uk/internet-grammar/.

It is also available on CD-ROM: details are given on the website.

Another internet source that provides information on grammar is the *AskOxford* website:

http://www.askoxford.com/.

Click on 'Ask the experts' and you are taken to a page where you can access 'frequently asked questions' (about grammar and other language matters), and 'jargon buster' (an A–Z glossary of grammatical terms). If you do not find your question answered on the website, there is a facility, at the bottom of the FAQ page, to submit your question to the experts at AskOxford.

Dictionaries

Every student should have a dictionary to hand for instant reference. You are recommended to have a desksize or concise edition, not anything smaller, such as a pocket or gem edition. Dictionaries often contain information over and above the description of words and definitions of their meanings. They may have geographical (place name) and biographical (people's names) entries. They may contain extensive notes on difficult and disputed usages of words. They may include an appendix on punctuation, or style, or tips on good writing. Modern dictionaries are usually available on CD-ROM, as well as in print versions; sometimes the CD-ROM is sold together with the print dictionary, sometimes separately.

A dictionary aimed specifically at students is the:

Encarta Student Dictionary, ISBN 0747562350

published in 2003 by Bloomsbury. Besides the usual dictionary information, it also includes:

- **quick facts: short digests of key concepts in the arts and sciences**
- **literary links: notes on major works of literature**
- **internet guide: on navigating and researching the internet**
- **warnings about spelling mistakes ignored by spellcheckers**

- commonly misspelled words

- usage notes covering common student problems with style, punctuation and grammar.

Also with the student in mind is the:

Collins English Dictionary Desktop Edition, ISBN 0007163347

published in 2004. This dictionary comes with a CD-ROM, containing numerous links to websites on the internet that provide further information about many of the headwords in the dictionary, especially the geographical and biographical entries. It also contains an extensive supplement, entitled 'Write on Target', which contains advice on writing essays, reports and CVs, and on giving presentations. The flagship of the Collins range is the desksize:

Collins English Dictionary, ISBN 0007197527

which is now in its sixth edition, 2003.

Probably the most well-known English dictionary is the *Concise Oxford Dictionary*. The current edition is the eleventh, published in 2004, and retitled:

Concise Oxford English Dictionary, ISBN 0198608640.

It uses a method of defining that was pioneered in its larger cousin, the desksize *New Oxford Dictionary of English*, originally published in 1998, but now in a second edition, 2003, under the title:

Oxford Dictionary of English, ISBN 0198613474.

The *Concise Oxford* also comes in a CD-ROM version, ISBN 0198610025. This edition of the *Concise* has a number of appendices containing a variety of additional information, including a 'Guide to Good English' with basic advice on grammar and punctuation.

The other major publisher of English dictionaries is Chambers, whose latest edition (2003) of their traditional, flagship dictionary is titled:

The Chambers Dictionary, ISBN 055010013X.

With a different layout and style of entry is the:

Chambers 21st Century Dictionary, ISBN 055014210X.

Originally published in 1996, this is available in a revised and updated edition from 1999, as well as on CD-ROM (ISBN 0550101365). It contains additional information on: spelling, grammar, idioms, word histories and pronunciation.

Some dictionary publishers allow free online access to one of their dictionaries, though not usually to their desksize products. Among those currently available are:

> *Chambers 21st Century Dictionary*: http://www.chambersharrap.co.uk/chambers/chref/chref.py/main
> *The Compact Oxford English Dictionary*: http://www.askoxford.com/dictionaries/
> *Merriam–Webster's 10th Edition*: http://www.m-w.com/ (access to the more up-to-date eleventh edition is by subscription).

It is sometimes the case that online versions of dictionaries are not the current edition. For access to sites that search multiple dictionaries, go to:

> http://www.onelook.com/
> http://www.yourdictionary.com/.

Usage Guides

Guides to problematical, disputed and variable usage in grammar and of words have a long pedigree. The two classics in the field are:

> H.W. Fowler's *Modern English Usage* (1926)
> Eric Partridge's *Usage and Abusage* (1942).

The latest (2004) edition of *Fowler's Modern English Usage* was revised by the former editor of the *Oxford English Dictionary*, the late R.W. Burchfield; and it is published by Oxford University Press (ISBN 0198610211). *Usage and Abusage* has been most recently (1999) revised by Janet Whitcut and published by Penguin Books (ISBN 0140514422).

Usage guides tend to be opinionated, over-prescriptive, and occasionally idiosyncratic. Neither Fowler nor Partridge, it must be said, falls into this category; though, in their original editions, they, naturally enough, reflected the prevailing usage of their time. Here is Fowler on 'between you and I':

> *Between you & I* is a piece of false grammar not sanctioned, like the contrary lapse *It is me*, even by colloquial usage; a similar lapse is seen in *It was a tragedy of this kind which brought home to my partner and I the necessity for* …

and on the difference between *until* and *till*:

> *Until* has very little of the archaic effect as compared with *till* that distinguishes *unto* from *to*, & substitution of it for *till* would seldom be noticeable, except in any such stereotyped phrase as *true till death*. Nevertheless, *till* is now the usual form, & *until* gives a certain leisurely or deliberate or pompous air; when the clause or phrase precedes the main sentence, *until* is perhaps actually the commoner (*until his accession he had been unpopular*).

The most comprehensive and well-grounded usage guide is:

> *The Cambridge Guide to English Usage*, ISBN 052162181X.

This guide, authored by Pam Peters of Macquarie University in Australia, was published by Cambridge University Press in 2004. It is based on computer corpora, as well as surveys of English speakers; and it reflects English usage around the world. Here is the *Cambridge Guide* on *till* and *until*, and *'til*:

> In most contexts **till** and **until** are equally good, witness:
>
> *The formalities can be delayed till they arrive.*
> *The formalities can be delayed until they arrive.*
>
> The extra syllable seems to make **until** a little more formal, though **till** is not an abbreviated form of it, but an independent older word. **Until** is however very much more common

in current English, outnumbering **till** by about 8:1 in BNC [British National Corpus] data and more than 30:1 in data from CCAE [Cambridge Corpus of American English] ... .

The form '**til** explains itself as an abbreviation of **until**, but is strictly redundant when **till** stands in its own right, as we have seen. In data from the BNC and CCAE, '**til** is used in quotations to suggest direct speech, as in 'the game ain't over 'til it's over'... But in both databases, '**til** with or without apostrophe is the least used of the three forms.

Not everyone will want this level of detail or be able to afford a usage guide of this size (600 + pages of large format). More handy, with good coverage and wittily written, is the late R.L. Trask's:

Mind the Gaffe – The Penguin Guide to Common Errors in English, ISBN 0140514767.

A paperback edition was published by Penguin Books in 2002. Here is Trask on *until* and *till*:

Both of these are perfectly acceptable, but standard English does not accept any of *til, *'*til* or *'*till*. And you should avoid the overly wordy **until such time as*: use *until* instead.

And here is Trask at his acerbic best:

communication This five-syllable word is hardly ever necessary, but it has become one of the great vogue words of our day. It has been pressed into service to mean everything from 'letter' or 'e-mail' on the one hand to 'public relations' or 'propaganda' on the other. Unless you are obliged to write vapid dross for a living, avoid this word except when you are certain that no other word can possibly express your meaning.

The internet has a number of sites, mostly American, that give advice on usage. They should be used with caution; the advice is often the personal opinion, or even hobby horse, of the website creator. The *AskOxford* site mentioned earlier may be used with confidence.

Style Guides

Publishers and news organisations usually issue a style guide for authors who write for them. Sometimes, this is just to ensure a consistent house style in the presentation of texts; but, for journalists, style guides contain quite detailed information on disputed and confusable usage, as well as advice on writing for their audience. The best known journalists' guides are:

> *The Economist Style Guide*, available at http://www.economist.co.uk/ research/styleguide/
> *The Guardian Style Guide*, available for consultation or download at http://www.guardian.co.uk/styleguide
> *The BBC News Style Guide*, downloadable as a PDF file at http://www.bbctraining.com/pdfs/newsStyleGuide.pdf.

The *Guardian* guide has also been published (2004) in a print version as:

> *The Guardian Stylebook*, ISBN 1843549913.

Attempts to persuade people, especially public communicators, to write more straightforwardly and simply have been led in recent years by The Plain English Campaign. One of the founders of that campaign, Martin Cutts, has written:

> *The Oxford Guide to Plain English*, ISBN 0198610114

published in an updated edition in 2004 by Oxford University Press. The Plain English Campaign also has a useful website:

> http://www.plainenglish.co.uk/index.html.

Another useful website and one of the best among a plethora of such American sites is Jack Lynch's

> *Guide to Grammar and Style*: http://www.andromeda.rutgers. edu/~jlynch/Writing/.

Jack Lynch is a member of staff of the English department at Rutgers University in Newark, New Jersey. He is an eighteenth century literature specialist; and he was one of the first to make material available on the internet for students of English language and literature.

Spelling

Where to find out about spelling? The obvious place to start is with a dictionary (see above). There are also specialised dictionaries of spelling, such as:

The Penguin Spelling Dictionary, ISBN 0140512306

published by Penguin Books in 1990.

If you want to understand some of the principles underlying the system of English spelling, you should consult a book written for teachers by John Mountford:

An Insight into English Spelling, ISBN 0340630949

published by Hodder & Stoughton in 1998.

An online help with spelling (and punctuation), including practice exercises, has been developed by the STELLA project in Glasgow University's School of English and Scottish Language and Literature, under the acronym ARIES (Assisted Revision in English Style), which can be accessed at:

http://projects.scottishcorpus.ac.uk/aries/.

Punctuation

For a straightforward and comprehensive account of punctuation, you can do no better than R.L. Trask's

The Penguin Guide to Punctuation, ISBN 0140513663

published by Penguin Books in 1997.

For an amusing, witty and occasionally opinionated account of punctuation you could read the book, with the subtitle 'The Zero Tolerance Approach to Punctuation', by Lynne Truss:

Eats, Shoots and Leaves, ISBN 1861976127

published by Profile Books in 2003.

The ARIES website, mentioned under 'Spelling', also contains advice and practice on punctuation.

EXERCISE

Pick up a good modern dictionary (one of those recommended above) and surprise yourself by finding out how much varied information about words it contains over and above the explanations of the meanings of words.

Glossary

Term	Chapter(s)	Definition/comment
		(Words in **bold** have an entry in the glossary.)
action	3	a type of situation, expressed by the **main verb**, in which a **subject** 'doer' instigates an action
active/passive	3, 4	a difference in the form of: (1) the **verb phrase**, e.g. *gave – was given*; (2) the sentence, in which a **transitive** structure of 'doer does victim' becomes 'victim is done by doer', e.g. *The student submitted the essay – The essay was submitted by the student*
additive connection	6	the mechanism for joining two sentences in which the second sentence adds information to the first, by means of **conjunctive adverbs** such as *moreover, furthermore, in other words*
adjectival clause	4	a type of **subordinate clause** that functions as a modifier of a noun; it may be a **finite relative clause** (e.g. *(the woman) who telephoned you*) or a **non-finite participle clause** (e.g. *(the woman) eating an ice-cream*)
adjective	2, 3	a class of words that function as modifiers of nouns, either before a noun (e.g. *the desirable outcome*), or after a verb like *be* (e.g. *this outcome was desirable*)

adjective phrase	2	a type of **phrase** whose headword is an adjective, which may be modified by an **intensifier** adverb (e.g. *very polite*) and/or a **prepositional phrase** (*very glad about the result*) or a **clause** (e.g. *glad that you are here, sure to know the answer*)
adverb	2, 3	a heterogeneous class of words, including **manner** adverbs (*politely*), time and place adverbs (*soon, here*), **conjunctive adverbs** (*nevertheless, therefore*)
adverb phrase	2	a type of phrase whose headword is an adverb, which may be preceded by an **intensifier** (e.g. *very well, quite suddenly*)
adverbial	3, 4	a **slot** in the structure of clauses/ sentences, filled by **circumstances** (of time, place, manner, reason, condition, etc.)
adverbial clause	3, 4	a type of **subordinate clause** that functions as **adverbial**, usually introduced by a **subordinating conjunction**
adversative connection	6	the mechanism for joining two sentences in which the second is in some way opposed to the first; signalled by **conjunctive adverbs** such as *however, nevertheless, yet*
apostrophe	9	a **punctuation** mark ('), used to signal possession (*the student's essay*), or an omitted letter (*don't, it's, we've*)
archaism	7	a word that sounds old-fashioned, e.g. *hereupon, spake, thrice*
auxiliary verb	2, 3	a small subclass of **verbs** that accompany **main verbs**; they include the **modal verbs**, as well as the verbs *be, have, do*
bad grammar	1	**sentence** structures that obscure the intended meaning, instead of making the **text** easy for the reader to understand

capital letter	9	in writing, a letter (A, B, C, etc.) used to begin a sentence and as the first letter of names of people, places, institutions, etc.
causal connection	6	the mechanism for joining two sentences in which the second follows logically from the first, signalled by **conjunctive adverbs** such as *consequently, therefore, and so*
circumstance	2, 3	an element of sentence structure expressing the accompanying context of an action, event or state, in relation to time, place, manner, reason, purpose, etc.
clause	2, 4	a unit with the same structure as a **simple sentence**, except that **non-finite subordinate clauses** may omit the **subject** element
cleft sentence	5	a mechanism for rearranging the elements of a sentence, by means of the formula '*It* + *be* + focus + relative clause' (e.g. *It was the Turkish Delight that I gave to her*)
collocation	3	the regular co-occurrence of two words in a lexical construction, e.g. *false* + *teeth, passport, number plate*, etc.
colon	9	a **punctuation** mark (:), used within a written sentence and usually followed by a list or an explanation of what precedes the colon
comma	1, 7, 8, 9	a **punctuation** mark (,), used to separate elements of a written sentence, to make the meaning clearer
complement	3, 4	a slot in the structure of **clauses/ sentences**, usually filled by an **adjective phrase** or **noun phrase**, which provides additional information about the **subject** or **object**
complex sentence	4	a sentence composed of a **main clause** and one or more **subordinate clauses**

compound	2	a word composed of two or more roots, which are usually independent words, e.g. *haircut*, *nail-biting*, *table manners*
compound sentence	4	a sentence composed of two or more **main clauses**, usually joined by a **co-ordinating conjunction**
condition circumstance	3	a circumstance usually expressed by an adverbial clause introduced by the subordinating conjunction *if*
conjunction	2, 9	a class of words that are used to join clauses together, e.g. *and, although, but, because*
conjunctive adverbs	6	a subclass of **adverbs** that are used to make connections between sentences, e.g. *however, moreover, therefore*
contractions	7	the shortening of either an **auxiliary verb** + *not* (e.g. *don't, isn't, mustn't*) or a **pronoun** + auxiliary verb (e.g. *she's, we've, they'd*)
co-ordinating conjunction	4, 6, 7	a subclass of **conjunctions** that are used to create **compound sentences**, and whose principal members are: *and, but, or*
countable/ uncountable	1	the distinction between **nouns** denoting things that may be counted (*boxes, ideas, parsnips*) and those that denote a 'mass' (*sloth, empathy, enthusiasm*)
criteria	1	the plural of *criterion*
dangling clause/phrase	7	a **clause** or **phrase** at the beginning of a **sentence** that does not relate to the following **subject** of the sentence
defining/ non-defining	1, 4, 7	used of **relative clauses**, and other modifiers of nouns, to distinguish those that 'define' which noun is being talked about from those that merely give additional information about it

determiner	2	a class of words that accompany nouns, including articles (*a*, *the*), **possessives** (*my*, *your*, *their*), and quantifiers (*several*, *ten*)
dialect	1	a variety of a language spoken in a particular geographical area or by a particular social group, e.g. Yorkshire dialect, teenage dialect
dictionary	10	a reference book that contains a selection from the vocabulary of a language and gives a variety of lexical information about its entries
different from/to	1	traditionally *from* is the 'correct' **preposition** after *different*, but *to* is more commonly used nowadays
direct object	4	the **slot** in **clause** structure that typically represents the 'victim' of an **action**
discourse	2	the term used to refer to speech organised as monologue or dialogue, by contrast with written **text**
embedded clause	4	another term for **subordinate clause**
essay	3	a written **text** that argues a thesis and is composed of **paragraphs** that develop the ongoing argument
event	3	a type of situation, represented by a **main verb**, in which something 'happens' without a human instigator
existential sentence	5	a sentence introduced by *there*, which states the existence of something
extraposition	5, 7	the delay of a **subject clause** to the end of the sentence, and its replacement by *it*
finite/non-finite	2, 4	the distinction in **clauses** and **verb phrases** between forms that show **tense** (*break*, *breaks*, *broke*) and those that do not (*breaking*, *broken*, *to break*)
fronting	5	placing an item in first position in a sentence that would not normally occupy it

given/new information	5	given information in a sentence has usually already been mentioned in the text, whereas new information is being mentioned for the first time
grammar	1, 8, 10	the system of rules/conventions for constructing sentences; the description of those **rules** in a book; the internalisation of those rules in the brain
grammar/style checker	8	a computer program incorporated in word processors, e.g. MS Word, that purport to offer advice on grammar and style – to be treated with extreme caution
homograph	2	words that are spelt the same, but are pronounced differently, e.g. *wind* (weather), *wind* (up)
homonym	2	different lexemes that are spelt and pronounced the same, e.g. *ear* (hearing), *ear* (of wheat or corn)
homophone	1, 9	words that are pronounced the same, but are spelt differently, e.g. *steel, steal*
however	1, 6	a **conjunctive adverb** indicating an **adversative connection**; it normally begins a sentence, or is the second element
hyphen	8, 9	a **punctuation** mark used to join elements of a **compound** word, e.g. *spoon-feed*; usage is variable
incomplete sentence	7	a 'sentence' that doesn't make sense as it stands, either because it is a **subordinate clause**, or because it lacks a **main verb**
indirect object	4	a **slot** in **clause** structure representing the recipient or beneficiary of an **action**
infinitive	2	a form of the **verb** usually introduced by *to*, e.g. *to spell, to leave*
infinitive clause	2, 4	a **subordinate clause** introduced by an **infinitive** form of the **verb**

inflections	1, 2	elements of words, usually suffixes, that signal grammatical meanings, e.g. plural of **nouns**, past tense of **verbs**
-ing clause	4	a type of **subordinate clause**, introduced by a **present participle** (*-ing*) form of a **verb**
intensifier	2	a subclass of **adverbs**, used to 'intensify' the meaning of **adjectives** or adverbs, e.g. *very*
it's	1, 7, 9	this form is only ever a contraction of *it is* or *it has*; it is not a possessive – which is spelt *its*
language change	7	this is inevitable, and at any time changes are in progress and lead to uncertainty about usage, e.g. *less* vs *fewer*
less/fewer	1, 7	traditionally, *fewer* is used with **countable nouns** (*fewer beefburgers*) and *less* with **uncountable** (*less salt*); but *less* is now regularly used with countable nouns
lexeme	2	a word viewed as a unit of vocabulary; the headwords in dictionaries; may have different grammatical forms; may be composed of more than one written **word**
main clause	4	the **clause** in a **complex sentence** to which **embedded clauses** are subordinate
main verb	2, 3	the last **verb** in a **verb phrase**, which provides the main reference of the **verb** element in a **clause**
manner circumstance	3	a **circumstance** slot filled by an element expressing the manner in which something is done or happens
modal verb	2	a subclass of **auxiliary verbs**, including *can, may, shall, will, must*, that occur as the first element in **verb phrases**
national curriculum	1	the curriculum specified for British schools by the Qualifications & Curriculum Authority

nominalisation	7	the derivation of **nouns** from **verbs**, e.g. *devolution* from *devolve*; overuse of this creates a style that is difficult to read
non-finite clause	2, 7	a **subordinate clause** introduced by a **non-finite** verb form (**infinitive** or **participle**)
non-standard	1	usage that does not conform to the norms of English used in written publications
noun	2, 3	a large class of words that denote persons, objects, substances, ideas, etc.
noun clause	4	a type of **subordinate clause** that occurs in **slots** in sentence structure that are normally filled by a **noun phrase**, e.g. **object**
noun modifier	2	a noun used with another noun, with a similar function to an **adjective**, e.g. *risk assessment*
noun phrase	2, 3, 4, 7	a type of phrase with a **noun** or **pronoun** as the headword and possibly containing **determiners**, **adjectives**, **relative clauses**, etc.
number/amount	1, 7	conventionally *number* is used with **countable** nouns (*a number of buses*) and *amount* with **uncountables** (*a large amount of traffic*); compare *less/fewer*
object	3, 4	the **slot** in **clause** structure that is usually filled by the 'victim' of an **action** (**direct object**) or the 'recipient' (**indirect object**)
object complement	4	a type of **complement** that relates to an **object**, e.g. *They have elected Bush president*
paragraph	2, 3, 6	a constituent element of a **text**, composed of sentences relating to a single topic
part of speech	2	an older term for **word class**
participle clause	1, 4	a **non-finite clause** introduced by a **present** or **past participle** form of a **verb**

passive sentence	3, 4, 5, 8	a sentence in which the 'victim' is in **subject** position, the **verb phrase** is in the passive form, and the 'doer' may be in a *by* phrase, e.g. *The painting was stolen by a professional gang*
past participle	2, 3	a **non-finite** form of the verb, usually with the suffix *-ed*, e.g. *followed, tasted, broken*
past tense	2	a **finite** form of the verb, usually with the suffix *-ed*, to denote past time, e.g. *laughed, sneezed, wrote*
phrasal verb	2	formed with a **verb** word + an **adverb** or **preposition**, e.g. *give in, look after*
phrase	2	a unit composed of words and functioning within a **slot** of **clause** structure
place circumstance	3	a **circumstance** slot filled by a place **adverbial**
possessive	2, 4	either a **determiner** (*my, your, our*, etc.) or a **pronoun** (*mine, yours, ours*, etc.), indicating possession
postponement	5	the movement of an element of sentence structure to the end of the sentence, which would not normally occupy that position
preposition	2, 7	a class of words used to join **noun phrases** to other sentence elements, e.g. *after, in, on, with*
prepositional phrase	2, 3	a phrase consisting of a **preposition** and a following **noun phrase**, e.g. *in the garage, with a computer*
present participle	2	a **non-finite** form of the **verb**, formed with the suffix *-ing*, e.g. *buying, singing, working*
present tense	2, 4	a **finite** form of the **verb** referring to habitual actions or timeless events and states, sometimes to present time, e.g. *float, floats, see, sees*

private state	3	a **state** that is experienced by a person or other animate being, e.g. *believe, hear, regret*
pronoun	2	a class of words whose function is to replace **noun phrases** in ongoing text, to avoid repetition, e.g. *you, she, they*
proofreading	8	the necessary task of checking your work for grammatical and spelling errors before you submit it, even if you have spellchecked it
punctuation	1, 9, 10	a system of marks used in writing to make the sense of a text clear to the reader
purpose circumstance	3	a **circumstance** slot in **clause** structure filled by a purpose **adverbial**, e.g. *(in order) to raise money*
quotation marks	9	a **punctuation** mark ('…')used for enclosing direct speech or quotation
rearrangement	5	altering the usual order of **sentence** elements to improve the flow of a **text**
reason circumstance	3	a **circumstance** slot in **clause** structure filled by a reason **adverbial,** e.g. *because the train was late*
relative clause	1, 2, 4, 5, 7, 8	a **subordinate clause** used to modify **nouns**, introduced by a relative **pronoun** (*who, whose, which, that*)
rules	1	the conventions for structuring **sentences** and **texts**
run-on sentence	7	two **main clauses** (sentences) separated only by a **comma** – to be avoided
semicolon	1, 9	a **punctuation** mark (;), used within **compound** and **complex sentences** to indicate how elements relate to each other
sentence	2, 3, 5, 6	a complete syntactic structure, composed of one or more **clauses**
simple sentence	2, 4	a sentence composed of a single **clause**
slot	2, 4	a position in **clause** structure, e.g. **subject, verb, object**, filled by a unit

word class	2	words grouped according to their **morphological** and **syntactic** features: **noun, verb, adjective, adverb, pronoun, determiner, preposition, conjunction**
word form	2	a word in a particular **inflectional** form, e.g. *trees* is the plural form of *tree*

Index